A NEW
PARENTS A ... UDENTS

COLLEGE

making the complicated

EASY →

RUSS VITALE

A NEW GUIDE FOR
PARENTS AND STUDENTS

College:
Making the *Complicated*
EASY

By Russ Vitale

"The Cool College Guy"

www.russvitalejustsayin.com

For college guidance and advice please follow Russ on Instagram: @thecollegeguy4you

thecollegeguy4you@gmail.com

Published by the Dream Keeper Foundation

Table of Contents

Dedication

I want to dedicate this book to my beautiful, smart and talented daughter who stood by me the entire way. Also, to the parents and students who helped make this book possible. And to my "assistant" for being my biggest fan.

Introduction

This book is about working hard, doing well, becoming informed to make good decisions, dreaming big, but also learning to adapt and find happiness wherever your college path may lead you. I can't promise admission or happiness unfortunately. However, I can help you understand how things may go, what you can do to properly prepare, how to avoid the big mistakes, and that life is not over if you or your student aren't admitted to their top choice school. In addition, I promise you that you won't be less successful, or fulfilled, as long as you (and you alone) don't allow your college destination to be the only thing that defines you.

I mean, why do we think all of the life dynamics that apply to everything we do if life won't, or shouldn't, apply to the college process?

I get that we all want our kids to get what they want, and hopefully they worked for it and deserve it. I am sure as a parent you have pushed your child to get the best grades possible and the best standardized tests scores possible, so they can get in to the "best" colleges possible. That's all well and good however whether you are starting the college application and admission process now (or will be in the near future), please understand that college is a journey, not a destination. I have seen this description many times over the years and it really is true.

If things go as you had hoped, with little modifications and smooth sailing, that is great! But the college process is usually fluid, constantly changing. It is how we collectively respond to this fluidity that can make a process much more complicated than it should be. This book is designed to give you the guidance and tools to react positively to the ever-changing journey. It is meant to help you make the complicated easy (or at least easier).

There are many books out there about college, the college process, how to find the "magical secrets" to get accepted into your top choice school, how to go through the process and not want to jump off a cliff midway through, and on and on. Not that these books aren't somewhat helpful, but this book is a little more realistic and reasonable in my opinion. It will help you regardless of your college aspirations, whether you are aiming for highly selective colleges or for colleges that are the right fit with no regard for what I call "bumper sticker envy".

You see, I've been advising students and their families for many years, helping them with their college process. I've spoken with, and provided thousands of families, guidance regarding their concerns, worries, and anxieties related to college. I've counseled, many students and their families, as they share their stories before, during and after their child starts their college journey. I have witnessed this firsthand. Many view their college success, or failure, on whether or not they were accepted to the schools expected. If it didn't go as they hoped, parents and students often feel that their future success is impossible to obtain. It is actually quite the opposite!

Observing the difference between how most people start this journey versus how it actually goes is primarily what drove me to write this book. I've seen the initial goals and expectations come to fruition but also crumble because many tend to be unrealistic.

This can happen, not because they or their student wasn't awesome, because in many cases they are, but because the process can be unkind.

I've had the privilege to get to know, and call my friends, some amazing young men and women (and their parents) over the years. These bonds and relationships have been created over time through the navigation of the uncertain and sometimes dangerous waters of the process.

We all believe our kids deserve the best, especially if they work hard, take the most rigorous classes, they are involved in great activities, and so on. But though their hard work is commendable, I know that they aren't guaranteed admission to their top choice school as a result of it. You know why? **Because the process colleges use is one of life's biggest mysteries**.

They don't share it, and often times no matter what your net result, you will most likely never know why you were, or were not, admitted to a specific college. So, what I teach my students and families, is to aim for colleges that they think are the best fit for them in every way, reaches, matches, and safeties. We will then work together to position them as best we can for admission. However, after we do our best, and agree it's our best, we need to let it go, knowing what we expect, but also that anything can happen.

I do have methods and experience that helps students and their families acquire a good understanding of what to expect as we go through the process. But most families understand that the process is subjective at times, and eventually they lower their resistance as we get closer to decision time, taking my advice and applying my philosophy on things. Most are joyous after they hear they were accepted to their top choice college. Others can be somewhat frustrated and confused if they weren't. But I promise they still have great options if they took, and followed, my advice. If they were active participants in the process, did what I suggested, and followed my advice and guidance, they know they did all they could, and it is not something they did that caused the outcome to not be what they hoped.

What bothers me most though, are the 10 to 15% of people I meet who just can't embrace the facts. It seems they would rather see themselves as failures than understand they (parents and students) will be every bit as successful as the next person, regardless of where they go to college.

If they take advantage of the resources, networking, and opportunities presented to them at the school they decide to attend, there is no limit to what they can achieve. Holding on for dear life to the potential to get admitted, even after being deferred or waitlisted, is something too many do. It may happen, but often it increases the stress, anxiety, and feelings of failure for everyone involved. My concern in this regard is that this behavior will set the foundation for how they may react to other things in their life. This book asks you to not let that happen.

There are many false claims made by others to improve your chances for admission and finding that secret formula. This book is not about that at all. This book is about aiming high (whatever that means for you), being proactive and being in the right mindset while going through the process.

I love what I do because I get to know today's youth. I consider myself lucky every day to work with these fine people, and it's what drives me, every day! We don't just talk about college admission, but also, we discuss life, as well as mental, academic, emotional, and physical preparedness. I have many students who I've helped go to high-end, selective schools and we celebrate them for sure. But we also celebrate the detours that take place. Though it can impact where a student may end up, witnessing how they have grown and developed over time from when we started working together, to the end of their journey, is great to watch and (better yet) be part of.

These are some of the greatest stories and victories that I share because they represent real life. And as I've said in many presentations, speaking engagements, consultations, and personal discussions, if you knew your child and family were going to be happy, right now, regardless of what their GPA was, SAT or ACT scores were, or where they went to college, wouldn't you sign up for that right now?

I know I would for my own daughter, the children of my friends and family, for my clients and for you.

School doesn't prepare us for all aspects of life. Formulas may help calculate certain things if you are in a field where that applies. However, most of us need grit, adaptability, the ability to pivot, and never-ending drive to accomplish our goals. If you can get past defining your success solely by the bumper sticker you have on your car, or the diploma that hangs on your wall, then you will get a lot out of this book and from the perspectives that I share.

No matter what college you attend, your college process is, and will be, what you make of it. Make it great no matter where you go to school!

"I wish you the best as well as much success and happiness throughout your college journey and beyond!!"

Russ

Getting Ready for Big Choices

"College is More than a Bumper Sticker."

Russ

I wrote this book to help provide advice for parents who want their children to enjoy college success. I also wrote this for teens needing to know more about the realities of the process. Therefore, this robust, yet simple and logical resource, does not attempt, or intend, to downplay the importance of competitive schools or standardized tests. However, the philosophy I share with my clients is to create a roadmap that leads them to the most successful outcome (for the student and family) regardless of the college(s) you are considering or your test scores.

My goal is to enable you to create your own roadmap, so you know what to do and when and how to do it. That way you can keep things in perspective and not weigh yourself down with unnecessary stress and anxiety. Regardless of where you are in the process, this book will help add clarity for you, and hopefully enable you to get reassurance that you are doing what you should be (and that things are going to turn out okay).

This simply means that I am asking you, as a parent, to stay open to the possibilities that college (as you may remember it) is somewhat different now.

Therefore, the way you went through the process of choosing a college may need to be adjusted.

Please be ready to let the "Cool College Guy" (That's a name I have acquired over the years created by my students) show you a new approach to choosing the best college(s) for you, so your child is positioned for future success and happiness. If you allow me to guide you, you will leave the skewed perceptions of others behind, and make what can be a complicated process a lot easier.

Another goal is to help you (student and parent) have an adjusted perception of the objectives of your college process. Many families incorrectly maintain that the goal is to get into the "best" college they can. That is because many parents and students have a perceived reality where they assume that the only way success can be achieved is if they go to a certain college. I have found this to not necessarily be true.

However, we will address many of these misperceptions throughout this book, so you can identify them specifically and make your own decisions. For example, many parents, and students, believe they should know their potential career choice before they apply to college. But that's not necessarily true. People also believe that if you major in an area that doesn't result in an immediate job, where you are earning lots of money, then you are wasting your time in college. This also has not proven to be true in my experience. You see the bragging rights on sport's sidelines, bumper stickers and watercooler talk are often what seem to fill parents and students with unrealistic expectations. When there are unrealistic expectations the results you achieve can be seen as disappointing.

So, it's that time, right? It's time for you (the student) and you (the parent) to have the talk about college. This is what you have been working for your whole academic career right? You are now ready to start the process of choosing which college is the right one.

This book will help you build the foundation you need for your application and admission success. I can help make the complicated easy.

Obviously, there are many dynamics to this process. But your end result, will be the best result, if you follow the guidance of this resource. I am not saying college is going to be easy. But I am saying that this book will help you go deeply into your search for the perfect college, and help you obtain the results that are best for you! By making smart choices now, you will fortify and strengthen your path, so you can get through the process with as little uncertainty, stress and pressure as possible.

As someone who attended college some time ago and now guides and advises high school students throughout their college application and admissions process, I've witnessed the fast changes that have taken place in the college arena firsthand. I have also spent a tremendous amount of time explaining to families how the underlying forces, and academic landscape in terms of competitiveness and admissibility, are evolving.

This is true relative to major selection and offerings, networking and support resources on campus, and the true correlation between reputation and college success. It is important to understand the new rules and atmosphere that exists in the college world, so you can make smart decisions. Many of these new dynamics I reveal to you in this book.

Through these many experiences, I have gained insight and I am happy to share it with you. I'll provide some information later on to help you get a better understanding of what you need to do to put yourself in the best position for college admission success.

If followed closely, this resource should help you find that success regardless of your final destination.

Over the years I have seen what I call the "after-market" results, as students I have worked with in the past come back to me, become my Facebook and LinkedIn friends (after they graduate high school).

I see them at concerts, sporting events, the gym, restaurants and Starbucks. When we talk they share their experiences and their current situation, which I very much take to heart. They responded to my unique approach that includes their mental, physical, emotional, and yes, educational needs and well-being. They have come to realize that all of these different variables impact their success in college. It is not just about their academic achievements that impact their overall experience. I cover many of these concepts within this book to help you get a true picture of what you can do to get through the process successfully, and happily, which I believe should be the main goal for every student and parent.

Here are some additional truths that college-bound families may want to consider as they go through the process. This comes from personal experience.

Pursuing a non-traditional career path, or one different from what was initially thought to be your major when you started the process, is absolutely fine and happens more often than most people think.

Choosing the right learning and social environment is much more important than the assumed prestige of a college based upon name recognition.

Balancing your workload (while in college) with opportunities provided by your college, such as clubs, sports, Greek life, etc., is a very important indicator of future success.

There is a difference between being challenged and being overwhelmed; choose challenged. One thing I see every day, is families making decisions throughout their journey based upon random expectations placed on the student.

These expectations, such as picking a school that is more academically challenging than the student can comfortably handle, can lead to a student not having the experience that they wanted.

Many students need to address these aspects one way or another. Many have either dealt with the consequences of these expectations, or realized early on that they needed to pivot, so they could confidently move forward with their college journey. While this is a part of life, keeping these expectations reasonable can provide a better outcome for all involved.

If you are a student reading this book, I encourage you to take a good inventory of your personal expectations, and how you can use college as a bridge to your best life, without worry of judgement. I know this is hard to do as your friends can't help but judge you and make comments. They still love you, but they just can't help themselves. It is just how it goes.

If you are a parent, I also encourage you to look at the total life experience your son or daughter will be part of during their college time. College is about academics, but it is also about their overall experience and being positioned for the next stage of their lives. The non-academic aspect of college is often the more lasting benefit (and effect) of going to college which makes your collective decision even more important.

Common Myths Surrounding the College Experience

There are many myths surrounding the "College Experience" that stem from a society obsessed with proving they are ahead of their neighbor. I am sure you know people like this right? This obsession can sometimes hinder the building of a bridge to the best of life. As a result, a negative outcome for the college student is possible. No one can deny that getting into a selective college is a great accomplishment. However, it's what you do while you are there, to position yourself for continued future prosperity that is the key.

So, to make sure you are using the right criteria to drive your decisions, I would like to share *5 common myths* with you, so we can discuss them and set the stage for the rest of this book.

1. Ivy League or "highly selective colleges" means a better education

2. A Championship Football Team guarantees a great experience

3. The weather will make me happy

4. Stronger name recognition equals better school

5. My parents went there, I should too.

So here we go, let's address one of these myths. Don't get me wrong, going to big-name school can be life-changing, it's true. However, so can any other school if it's the right environment for the student. With a big sports program sometimes comes larger classes, less guidance when difficulty strikes and exposure to things requiring good decision-making skills.

That's not to say that it isn't exciting to have your team in the NCAA Basketball Tournament. But in my opinion, that should not be a driving factor for making a decision to apply or attend a college. This is high level, of course, and we will get into it in greater detail throughout the book. However, I wanted to share why these are myths versus actual truths.

To further test my theory, I recently had the opportunity to speak with a friend of mine, who sent his children to Ivy League colleges. His response confirmed what I was thinking all along: The bumper sticker of a highly selective college is not enough to automatically graduate and become a success in life. Two of his kids struggled finding jobs after graduation. One actually worked in a restaurant as a waitress until she found a job.

There is nothing wrong with this and actually, I did the same. But, I am sure neither the student nor the parent, expected this to be the case when they were accepted to this Ivy League college. In my work, I have seen just as many students succeed after graduating from schools that hardly anybody knows, as those who graduate from brand name colleges. The same life dynamics for potential success and happiness apply to all colleges. No school or person is immune.

I feel keeping the right perspective is a family responsibility. The students have an obligation to themselves to make the best choice. In turn, parents also have an obligation to help the student decide on what is best for them despite the name (brand) that is attached to it.

We need to have a mindset that helps us always live in a state of readiness. We need to be ready to take advantage of the opportunities that come our way.

Ready to address the challenges we face, and ready to live the life we were meant to live. To me the college process is a prime example of this concept.

"If I can help just one family, or student, avoid feeling like they have failed because things didn't go exactly as planned on their college journey, then that makes it all worthwhile. It makes me very proud of my occupation."

Russ

I've worked with hundreds of students, at all academic abilities and levels. I have also seen many teens struggle, and not enjoy their best life, because they come out of college exhausted and disenchanted. Kids are often tossed around in this decision and end up going to a college for reasons that don't include what is best for their future happiness. What the family thought was the best choice, became an ongoing struggle later on. This is so important to discuss right up front because it can happen anywhere, to anyone. However, this choice must be made after taking some action steps during the decision-making process to try to mitigate the potential for a negative experience. We will discuss this further in this book, so you can hopefully aim high, but also keep a healthy perspective.

The Choice Should Always Include Potential Happiness

I know this sounds non-academic, and it is. But we need to understand that college, and life, is not all about academics. The choices that parents (and teens) make, impact their lives, not just an education.

I strive, every day, to show parents and students that their choices must be well-rounded for the student and the family.

Many therefore consider colleges that were not originally on their radar. There are many times when their initial reaction to a particular school may not start out to be very supportive. Many students and families don't know much about specific colleges and even majors until I introduce them. If they maintain an open mind and keep what is in the best interest of the student at the forefront, the outcome will be a good one.

I get many "thank you" sentiments after the student has begun their college journey at a school I suggested. And they are thriving! This is among the most satisfying aspects of my business.

While sharing thoughts regarding the decisions kids and parents make, I often think to myself "Is our goal to push kids to go to a school where they may be unhappy just because the name is "impressive"? And impressive to whom? If we know that they may never cross the bridge to their best life, or may end up hating what they are doing, is it really worth it?

As an adult, how many of your family or friends do you know who feel this way and struggle with this dilemma? I know there is no guarantee, but again, there have been many experiences where I have witnessed decisions being made, sometimes not for the best reasons. This has convinced me that writing this book filled with resources and candid real talk, was the best decision I could have made!

But really, I share this with you because I approach the parents and teens I advise as if they were part of my family. I always consider what I would do with my own daughter as I guide them.

They obviously may have different abilities, goals, competencies, dreams, strengths, weaknesses, insecurities, personalities, and so on.

But over the years, I have encountered just about every scenario you can imagine. So, I am comfortable sharing my experiences, learning as much as I can about their specific situation or circumstance, and advising them accordingly. What I share in this book comes from these many experiences working with a wide variety of families with very diverse goals.

Getting these families, and now you, to understand all the factors that impact your decision and who the student really is, has become my talent - *Super Power* if you will. (Okay so, full disclosure here, Thor is my favorite super hero. Though my daughter bought me his hammer, it appears it doesn't work the same for me. Therefore, I have decided my *ability to relate and build trust with my students and parents* is my true *Super Power*. Not as flashy as the hammer I know, but more impactful in my opinion).

How I can connect with my students, to become their confidant and advocate is what drives me. That's why they come back to see me and say they miss me when they go off to college or are finishing high school. They come by just to say hello despite not having any need for additional college guidance because they know I have taken the time to really know them. I support them (100%) for who they are and who they want to be, but I am also direct and fair if they aren't doing what they are capable of.

This is one of the most satisfying parts of my business, and it is one of the biggest reasons I started on this path. It's what I pride myself in being, and doing, every day. It's why I say that I love every day and what I do. I know I can impact every single family, every single child/student I work with in a positive way, and this book aims to do the same for you.

I am walking proof that you can take a non-traditional path in almost every aspect of your life, and still end up happy, provide a positive influence and be okay. And that's what I want my students to know. They need to understand that often life is not a direct line between what you want, and how you get there, and it should not be expected to be so.

Taking an alternative path is not failure, but quite the opposite. It's navigating your life based upon the opportunities, and challenges, that come your way, and learning to pivot so you make the most of them. If you approach them this way you will not let the unexpected derail your mission for happiness and success. Pivoting is a life skill and something I discuss in detail with all of my students.

So, for you, a parent like me, I want to see you and your child have a balanced experience. I want your child to do the work necessary to find their way through the new college world with confidence and courage.

As your "Cool College Guy" extended family member, I want to share my approach with you so when the time comes, you are armed with knowledge that will support all of you in the decisions needed to be made along the way.

ATTENTION: YOU CAN ENJOY THIS PROCESS RATHER THAN HOPING IT WAS OVER!

My goal is to help provide insight, so you can feel what it really should be.

I want you to be able to take a deep breath remembering it's about your child, not the perceived prestige of a place, aka "Bumper Sticker Envy".

There are many ways to go through this part of their life, and one is not necessarily any better than the other. They can be successful, and happy, no matter where their journey takes them. At the end of the day, as parents, don't we just want our kids to be happy? Wouldn't you want your child to go to a place that makes them happy and provides them with the best opportunity for success?

Imagine how much of your thoughts and energy go into thinking about your child's well-being on a regular basis. A friend of mine once said, "You know Russ, as a parent, you're only as happy as your least happy child". It resonated with me and I thought of my daughter. For many years, I've worked with many families with multiple children, and I've seen it in action.

I want to help you with this part of your life so that the bridge to happiness, and being okay, is strong and direct. For everyone's sake, and to benefit your family, I want to be able to show you that despite the road that you may travel, and the detours you may face, there are always alternate routes to ensure your well-being, success and happiness.

Regardless of your child's college ambitions, this book will help you gain clarity on what needs to be done and when. Regardless of the academic ability and performance of your child, this book will do the same. Regardless of what your thoughts are if you are a parent, this book will provide perspectives that will enable you to support your child and help them throughout a process that can be very stressful and filled with pressure.

The Complicated Process Can Be Made Easy.

Here's How.

Russ' Rules… For Staying Cool

1. **The process doesn't have to be complicated.**

   There are many ongoing aspects of the process that, at times, may overwhelm and challenge you as a family. Please do your best to not get pressured to do things you shouldn't, and take a break when things start getting out of control. It will help you and your family. Slow down and think clearly about how you can address the current challenge. Ask yourself if the overall impact really is as great as you may think it is at the moment, or are you getting caught up in it because it is a variation from what you expected?

2. **The road to your final college destination is not always going to be a straight line.**

   As with life, there are always things that are unexpected that can derail your mission if you let them. Don't allow this to happen. Proper planning and understanding what to do and when can absolutely improve your chances for getting the results you desire. However, being flexible, and being able to pivot when needed, is key to managing the process successfully, and maintaining your sanity. By applying my philosophy and tips to your process, you can stay on your current path but also can enjoy opportunities you never thought possible.

Surprisingly, they may even be better than what you originally thought you wanted.

3. **Understand that the college process is not about "Bumper Sticker Envy"**

> At the forefront of every decision you make, for the best return on investment (meaning your child's time, effort and peace-of-mind as well as the money you have and will spend to support your child throughout the process) it is important to understand the type of person your student is, and how they react to different environments.
>
> Keep their personal happiness and success as key factors. Aim for them to push themselves to be their best, but realize that pushing them to impress your neighbors and family can have a negative impact on the student, their future success and their future happiness.

Formula For Being a Successful "College-Bound" Parent

1. Regardless of my **Child's** final test scores, cumulative GPA, or **college attended**, I will let him/her know that I **Love** them and that I am **Proud** of them.

2. College is the intersection of **Student Academics** and **Family Finance**. I am not afraid to reasonably, not excessively, invest in my **Child** (Time, Test Prep, Visitation Costs, etc). Our **Family's** college expenses will be one of the largest investments in our financial lifetime. Therefore, the investment I make in College Planning cannot only produce spectacular results for my **Child** but may also result in considerable savings for my **Family**.

3. As a **PARENT** I need to maximize the opportunities presented to us during the high school years. Therefore, we need to start early, make time to maximize the time we have left and engage professionals to help us make solid **Family** decisions if needed.

4. I will make it a point to ask questions, attend events, and learn about the **College Process** from multiple sources. However, I will only act upon information I gather if it applies to our situation and is in line with the goals, abilities and happiness quotients of my **Child** – I will avoid potentially inaccurate, damaging advice.

5. I don't compare my **Child** to his/her peers or siblings in front of them. We are all different. Our goal is to support our **Child** so we can maximize the opportunity to position them for success in college and in life.

6. I CANNOT expect a 15, 16, 17, 18 year-old **Student** to be wise enough, mature enough or worldly enough to drive the College Planning Process alone.

7. I need to be in charge (but not overwhelming), know we are a team, delegate responsibilities as needed to my **Child** and realize choosing a college is a **Family Decision**.

8. I will ask for help as needed from resources I trust but despite this fact I have no obligation to act upon that person's information unless it is in the best interest of my **Student** and **Family**.

9. I listen politely to other **Parents** regarding their College Process, but I must keep in mind, that although they usually mean well, they are not professionals, often have their details confused and/or their experience may be completely different from ours.

10. I will not rely solely upon my **Child's** teachers, school, or guidance counselor. However, they can be great resources and a great compliment to the college team I assemble to build our **Family's** college plan.

11. I have a **RIGHT** to expect *hard work* from my **Student**. Truth be told, there are few kids that "test well", but there are many kids that practice, prep, and sit for repeated test dates. The kid who "leaves nothing" on the wrestling mat, the volleyball court, the lacrosse field, the theatrical stage, the ensemble practice, and the practice test, has earned their CONFIDENCE regardless of the outcome.

Formula For Being a Successful "College-Bound" Student

1. Regardless of my final test scores, cumulative GPA, or **college attended**, I will know that my Parents **Love** me and are **Proud** of me.

2. College is the intersection of **Student Academics** and **Family Finance**. I realize that college is expensive as is the preparation that goes into it (Time, Test Prep, Visitation Costs, etc). College will be one of the largest investments in my Parent's financial lifetime. Therefore, I will do everything I can to produce spectacular results and do my part to increase my potential for considerable savings for my **Family**.

3. As a **STUDENT** I need to maximize the opportunities presented to me during my high school years. Therefore, I need to start early, make time to maximize my results and let my **Family** know if help is needed.

4. I will make it a point to ask questions, attend events, and learn about the **College Process** from multiple sources. However, I will only act upon information I gather if it applies to my situation and is in line with my goals, abilities and happiness quotients and is approved by my **Parents**.

5. I know this is a stressful time for my **Parents** as well. Their goal is to support me but I need to do my part so I can maximize the opportunity to position myself for success in college and in life.

6. I CANNOT expect my **Parents** to drive the College Planning Process alone. I need to be in charge (but not become overwhelmed), know we are a team, ask for help as needed and realize choosing a college is a **Family Decision**.

7. I will ask for help as needed from resources I trust but despite this fact I have no obligation to act upon that person's information unless it is in the best interest of me, my goals and my **Family**.

8. I listen politely to other **Parents and Students** regarding their College Process, but I must keep in mind, that although they usually mean well, they are not professionals, often have their details confused and/or their experience may be completely different from mine.

9. I will not rely solely upon my teachers, school, or guidance counselor. However, they can be great resources and a great compliment to the college team I assemble to build our **Family's** college plan.

10. My **Parents** have a **RIGHT** to expect *hard work* from me. Truth be told, I know I will need to practice, prep, and sit for repeated test dates. I need to "leave nothing" on the wrestling mat, the volleyball court, the lacrosse field, the theatrical stage, the ensemble practice, and the **College Process** so I can produce the best outcome possible for me and my **Family**.

By Russ Vitale "The Cool College Guy"

Finding the Right Mindset

"Are You a Squirrel or a Manatee?"

Russ

The College Entry Process

The college entry process is one that can be filled with uncertainty and anxiety as well as tremendous pressure on all levels; mental, physical and emotional. However, it doesn't need to be that way. My approach has always been to push my students to be their best but also to enable them to accept that wherever they are they will always be okay. I'm direct but not a dream crusher.

This means that I always tell them my honest opinion while listening to what they dream of doing. If we can find a happy balance, then I feel that we have done what we can to provide the guidance they need while also supporting them in their often lofty goals.

That being said, getting to this place can be challenging at times. It's not always simple. However, we can make it worse with our reactions to things that don't go as planned and with how we manage things as we go through the process. So, in an attempt to make the complicated process of college a little less so, understanding the two very different personalities that people may possess while navigating their journey, I have created this *Squirrel* and *Manatee* analogy. Let me explain.

"The Squirrel"

As a driver or passenger, seeing a squirrel in the middle of the road doing its panicked gyrations as you approach it can be stressful. Of course, you don't want to hit the poor little guy, but you sure do not want to hit other vehicles, a tree or run your car off the road trying to figure out where the squirrel will move next. No matter your opinion on squirrels, you have to admit that at first glance they are kind of cute. I say this even after my event at the US Open in Queens, New York some years ago when I thought I was about to have a relaxing and downright, let's just say, potentially romantic candle-light dinner before the tennis matches started only to be terrorized by a demon squirrel who apparently was part Italian.

It was obvious he was hungry, and he was also very persistent, and apparently on a mission to take my supper consisting of Sopressata, Prosciutto and Provolone right from my hands if he could. It ended up being a funny story about the "Squirrel from Queens" with a craving for Italian food, but it was somewhat scary at first. Despite this experience, I still think squirrels are cute at first glance.

Getting back to the "Squirrel" analogy, many people go through life just like a squirrel, moving from side to side, seeming to be overwhelmed with potential options and making the choice of which path to take – only when it's almost too late.

Some of you may be this type of person, and we all know someone who is. In fact, my best friend has acquired the name "Squirrel". Of course, this is meant affectionately because she is always going 90 miles an hour from one topic to the next and sometimes you are dizzy trying to keep up.

I mean, she is good at it, going from question to question while smiling and not even taking a single breath!

I find it entertaining, and because I am the "Cool College Guy" I love to find constructive humor in life. I am one of the few who can follow my friend "Squirrel" through 12 topic changes and 14 questions in 2 minutes. Most people are like, "Wait. Can we go back to the first thing you said?"

This can be the same in the fast-paced reality of making decisions and dealing with all the information, rumors and myths surrounding the college process. However, armed with the right tools, you (the student) or, you (the parent) can glide through the process without much trouble. Learning how to be both a squirrel (when needed) and manatee (when needed) will help you make the complicated process, easy.

We will get to the manatee shortly but first.......

It's okay to be a "Squirrel"

My friend "Squirrel" is an amazing friend and her intentions are of the highest level. She is this way because she cares about the outcome so much, not for herself, but for others. I feel most squirrels are pretty smart and this causes their minds to zip at high-speed trying to account for every possible outcome to ensure a desired result is met.

Technology and social communication have caused most people today, to have a quick mindset. In an attempt to have the right college experience, remember that you can make a fast decision, and a good decision at the same time.

But also remember, that in most cases the sense of urgency isn't as great as we sometimes make it out to be and the overall impact of the decision probably won't be the reason a student is or isn't accepted to their top choice school, just sayin'.

Often parents can tend to lean more towards the squirrel side of things, often overwhelmed and so interested in having the best outcome for their child that they can get a little carried away at times. But rest assured students, it is the "Squirrel" behavior from your parents that is often the reason things get done so it is nice at times to have a squirrel for a parent.

The "Manatee"

Then there's the manatee. Also, cute, but in a much different way. Manatees happen to be one of my daughter's favorite animals. She has wanted one for years and needless to say that isn't happening.

These anonymous animals move slowly and float through the water in what seems to be no particular hurry. It is fun to watch but it also can be frustrating to watch the slowness of a manatee. This is true especially if you happen to be a "Squirrel".

I have another friend and he's got the "Manatee" down pat. Nothing seems to upset him ever. The house could be on fire and he would say, "Okay hold on a second. Don't rush me, I just need to get my shoes on and then I'll be out there with you."

People who behave as "Manatees" can be frustrating as well because you really want them to share your panic, worry, anxiety and despair yet they mosey along as if nothing is happening and act like they "know" everything will be okay.

If you are a parent, you may feel this way often when you interact with your kids.

Now, people who are this way are not lazy or unintelligent, they simply process things differently. They most likely have different expectations or assume all is manageable no matter what the circumstances are. In a way, it's kind of nice to see that someone can just roll with things and not overreact to every action or inaction, isn't it?

The Best Blend

When it comes to college planning and life, if you're a "Squirrel" you will likely cause much more work than is necessary. You're also likely to cause your family and yourself much more busywork and potential stress than is warranted for the given situation. If you are "Manatee" you will most likely be much more relaxed and more likely to miss deadlines, not implement strategies to optimize results and/or settle for something less than what was originally possible.

The Cool College Guy thinks it's important to be both at certain times and it's even more important to know when to be one versus the other. Again there's no one way to go through the college process or life for that matter. But knowing when it's time to flip the switch and therefore your mode from one to the next is critical to surviving and dare I say, potentially enjoying the process.

Finding the Right "Squirrel/Manatee" Mix.

Try the Following Steps:

1. **Decide if you want to be more like a "Squirrel" or "Manatee", and then react accordingly.**

   Levity and lighthearted understanding of your shortcomings and strengths can go a long way when it comes to the college process. Plus, check the impact you're having on those around you. Be a "Squirrel" when it helps alleviate the stress you and your family are feeling. However, be the "Manatee" when surrounded by "Squirrels" by taking a calm, relaxed approach as needed to help the situation. You can make this process easy and not complicated with practice.

2. **Identify the things that need to be done and tag them as "Squirrel" or "Manatee" events, so you know the timing and urgency of each, as well as when something is going to change from "Manatee" to "Squirrel" mode and vice versa.**

   Not everything can be or needs to be a "Squirrel" event. Some things, though important, can wait to be decided. Time is a valuable asset for sure; we need to optimize our time with all we do. However, allowing things to run their course is also important and sometimes you run into experiences that require time to find the right way to act or react.

3. **Dismiss the rumors, myths and hearsay of others.**

> Many people offer their opinions even if you don't ask for them. Sometimes this is an effort to help, but many times it is just to show people what they "think they know". Sometimes it is hard to know the difference. I always ask my students, clients and parents, "What myth can I address with you today?" and "How can I give you the answers you have been looking for and the clarity and guidance you need?" This is really important because it's easy to get turned into "Squirrel" mode or "Manatee" mode with artificial intelligence, and this means "False Facts". Your situation is unique to you. Listen to tips and advice if you think they might be helpful. But before you take action, validate that the assumptions you're making are actually true and/or that they really apply to you.

4. **Take action.**

> Once you have categorized the "Squirrel" and "Manatee" items, start doing things to address them, get educated on each and then reevaluate to see if they still belong in the same category. This should be done keeping your specific goals in mind and applicability to your situation. Upon determining this fact, move on, get information, ask questions and determine your next steps (if any) so the item can be completed, moved to another classification or time period, or omitted completely.

5. **The specific college calendar remains relatively constant year after year for every student.**

> For example, November 1 is what is called an "Early Action" or "Early Decision Day for many colleges. No matter what you do you're not going to be able to change this date. So, if you are going to apply to a school using one of these admissions strategies you will be held to this date whether you like it or not. Repeat after me: November 1 is a big Early Decision and Early Action date. Your admission strategy may change, test scores may change, as may the list of schools you are interested in. Keep flexible throughout the process but know the deadlines and plan accordingly. This is a prime example of when being a "Manatee" (student) can catch up with you. It is also a good example of when the "Squirrel" tendencies reach their peak as parents start panicking that the date will be missed.

6. **Change is okay.**

> Often times change is better for a person. Even though the impact of notification that the student is either accepted, waitlisted, deferred or (gulp) rejected is still important, it is key to not overreact. Whether you are a "Squirrel" or "Manatee", self-awareness, as well as bulking together categories of events and situations as either a *"Squirrel"* or a *"Manatee"* event is critical in creating the right behaviors and responses. A team of all "Squirrels" is likely to not enjoy the process, even if the outcome

happens to be the one they desired. A team of only "Manatees" are likely to miss opportunities for optimizing the options available to them and they may even harbor feelings of regret – even when the outcome is deemed acceptable.

I told you the story of a "Squirrel and a Manatee" to emphasize the importance of having a good balance of personality and behavioral techniques in place as you (the Parent) or you (the Student) work toward making the complicated easy in this process.

Taking these steps will help you to make better decisions, help instill a feeling of calmness (I hope) and provide you with a better understanding of how you react in different situations, so you can stay on the easy track.

Russ' Rules... For Staying Cool

1. **Identify the key people in your college process as either "Squirrels" or "Manatees".**

   This is important, so you know what to expect as you go through the process. Try not to be upset with them for being as they are but understand so you know how to interact with them and how to react when things start going differently than expected (which will happen to everyone in some capacity).

2. **Tag the action that needs to be taken as either "Squirrel" or "Manatee" items and proceed accordingly.**

   Not everything can be or needs to be a "Squirrel" event. For example, preparing for the SAT or ACT, writing essays or finalizing the college list, are all examples of things you need to be aware of and plan for. However, you can't rush them! There is a process, learning and trial and error that needs to take place over time. Being a "Squirrel" with these things will only increase the stress level of all involved. Where you are in the college calendar obviously can impact the event categorization. If you have started, allowing yourself ample time to get things done, you will know which event is a "Squirrel" event and which is a "Manatee" event.

3. **Know that the process will require both the "Squirrel" and "Manatee".**

There will be times that you will need to be both. The process, as structured as it can be on one hand, is fluid in many ways. Finding the right balance is going to help the family dynamic stay calm. One of the most common compliments I get as I work with families is that they always feel better after they leave my office. It is largely because I tell my clients we can and will handle anything that comes up, all is doable.

We assess the challenges and status, identify steps to take to ensure we are where we need to be and then talk about what is on the horizon, so we are all on the same page and can plan accordingly. Hopefully keeping the right balance of "Squirrel" and "Manatee", as well as following what's in this book will allow you to feel the same.

By Russ Vitale "The Cool College Guy"

Ready, Set, Go!

"When in doubt, start now!"

Russ

My summers in high school and college consisted of mowing more grass than I wished to see on a weekly basis and an occasional patio deck or lawn sprinkler project. I remember that these projects were a welcomed break from riding on top of the truck which was allowed in those days (and I would never recommend you doing this now) and racing from house to house to get as many lawns done as possible. However, when we were about to start these welcomed projects and we saw all the wood laying around, or the plastic hoses, my friends and I would stare at each other and say, "Where should we start?"

We all knew what we were doing, and what we needed to be doing, but we had no idea where to start because it looked overwhelming and getting started was ominous. Anticipating the effort and potential challenges we would face weighed heavy on our minds. Similarly, starting the college process can cause discomfort. You know what I mean? You know you want to go to college but have no idea where to start. You know you should start your child on the process but with all you have going on and all the information you have, what do you do and when do you do it?

That's where I come in and where this book will help you.

The "Cool College Guy" spends his days helping families find the best way to start and make progress through the process in a way that is manageable and less stressful than most experience (remember, stressed spelled backwards is desserts. Now that is something much easier to dive into, right?)

So far, we have talked about the mindset you should try to be in when thinking about colleges for you or your student. Now we are going to shift gears to talk about planning the process, so you can get going, not be overwhelmed and can feel confident that you are doing what is needed to make solid decisions.

Really, any new endeavor can seem overwhelming. Thinking about where to start the college process is like planning a trip or cruise; you know where you want to go, or think you do, but have no idea where to start. Not knowing where to start your trip, could impact things like timing, availability and cost. The same is true with the college planning process. Before you know it, it becomes a belabored process where your confusion is increased. We want to avoid this at all costs.

Now, the more flexible you can be, the more options you will have with the college process. For example, if you started early summer of your sophomore year of high school you have much more flexibility to get things done and make progress at a less stressful pace. In contrast, if you are now a junior in the "May or June" timeframe of your junior year, it will be more important to be efficient with where and how you begin the process. In addition, what you get done each week to ensure you are exploring all options, maximizing your potential to get accepted to the school(s) you are interested in and to get the things done that you need to do, such as college visits and essays without making it a high anxiety event will need to be addressed.

"Other than money, the most vital asset we have is time."

Russ

I tell every family I work with this important statement. This theory applies to college but also applies to life as well: most of us adults know that. With two working parents, single parents, divorced parents, multiple kids, athletic schedules, work schedules, travel, etc., it is easy to find a million reasons why you can't fit in some "time" to start now. As a result, you start rationalizing in your mind that you can start next week or next month. Though I get that, and I often have many things on my plate daily as well, I can assure you the BEST time to start is now!!

I believe this message is so important that I have several presentations that I do for prospective clients, athletic booster clubs, different parent organizations and others called, "The Road to College Starts Now!!" It is not to scare people, but it is to create a sense of urgency. We all know that we tend to react more and better when there's some kind of emotional tie to what we're doing.

By causing an emotional reaction, it is intended to hit a cord to cause them to think about college NOW!!!!! I am sure some people are intimidated by the title and may be hesitant to attend but honestly, I want to get your attention and let you know, especially after reading this book, if you follow my advice, break things down into manageable chunks, take action and keep a reasonable perspective, you can do this!

Think about it, college is potentially one of the most important, uncertain, stressful and expensive parts of your life. Kids and parents get overwhelmed with information. Some information they receive is unsolicited, especially after you take your first PSAT. Some people actually think they are doing their research and becoming educated as they receive mail and get notices from their school.

This may help a little, but some overwhelm themselves with information and don't know which contradictory information they should follow. It is kind of like trying to take a sip of water out of a firehose. Once again, I say take a deep breath, break everything down in small, manageable chunks, understand what applies to you and what doesn't, and then start taking action based upon your needs and that of your student. Don't worry about what everyone else is doing, or not doing. Both can either cause you much unnecessary stress while the other can lure you into a place of inaction.

I'd also like to address another thing that comes up as I consult and advise clients as they start the process; most kids aren't lazy! I mean some may be, but a majority are not at all. However, they are sometimes not motivated because, like many parents, they are overwhelmed by the choices, don't want to disappoint their parents, have way too many things taking up their time and they don't know where to start. Many psychologists I know say that most kids know in general what they have to do, but it's too big of an unknown, so they go into a turtle mode and withdraw into a shell.

When I say "most kids" this is where I am speaking to all of the teens who choose to go with the crowd, rather than choose to create their own journey. The kids who think if they ignore it long enough, it will go away. I never reprimand kids I work with for feeling this way or for their inaction. Instead, I defend them. I let them know I understand why they feel the way they do, and I want to help them move forward without pressure and stress. Nine times out of ten I can tell you their shoulders come back down where they belong, they start to breathe normally, and I see a liveliness in their eyes saying, "Thank you for understanding and believing in me." That's when I know we are ready to really rock and roll.

I know I can help you come out of "turtle and herd mode" because I have a way to encourage movement. It doesn't matter if you have high-end aspirations for yourself or your kids, or if your goals end up being just getting to the "right place" (which is the real goal in my opinion, but what do I know?), the process has so many moving parts and they can seem complex. There are many things that need to get done and as students and parents you are told all kinds of inaccurate things that sound convincing.

This again forces you into inaction rather than action. The uncertainty increases, you argue at home and sweep the topic under the mat saying that you will discuss it another time. It doesn't matter if the information you receive comes from your friends, peers, family, teachers, whomever. I am asking you to follow your own path, don't worry about the past and look forward to creating the best outcome possible for you and your family. It is not a race as the well-known movie *Race to Nowhere* clearly states in its title. A must see by the way if you haven't seen it.

One of my favorite flashbacks that I like to share with my students and parents who feel they are behind in starting their college process or haven't accomplished what they hoped for academically comes from one of my favorite animated movies *The Lion King*.[i] Before you roll your eyes, keep reading and hear what I am saying please.

Anyway, there is a scene in the movie after Rafiki learns that Simba is still alive. They meet and have a pointed discussion in the middle of high grasses. Rafiki tells Simba he needs to come back to Pride Rock because his uncle has ruined everything, and they are in big trouble. This angers Simba, but he gets in his own head and starts rattling off all the reasons he can't come back. One excuse after another. Well Rafiki finally has enough and he rears back and hits Simba in the head with his long, hard wooden staff. Simba gets dazed a bit and asks, "What was that for?" Rafiki calmly looks right at him and says, "It doesn't matter, it's in the past."

I share this with students because it doesn't matter if we are discussing standardized testing or trials and tribulations of the transcript or past acceptances and rejections of people they know at colleges they are considering; the past is only one criterion we use to try to evaluate things. In my opinion, the past should never be the thing that stops us from doing our best, showing improvement and/or pursuing our goals and dreams.

So, when you get overwhelmed with doubt and start making excuses why things aren't going to work out, stop! Think about the conversation Simba had and how he needed a little help but finally realized the past is just that, the past, and the **future is for you to create and pursue.**

> *Unfortunately, all the information that you gather from multiple sources, credible and not-so-much, tends to intimidate a lot of kids and make them worry about their own college journey. In reality, most of what they hear from others is not accurate at all, doesn't apply to them or even if has the potential to be accurate at the moment, it is not something they need to worry about now.*

So, despite the great challenges you might anticipate in the college process, which can have significant impact on the student and their family, stay true to yourself and what you really want in a college experience. Don't let feeling overwhelmed cause you to make very wrong choices. I always strive to show all my clients the individual choices available to them, so they can go outside of the box. This way they can create a unique college experience, customize their plan based upon the student and family needs, and make the most of the time they have in front of them.

Here's How to Take Action Now

Pick a weekend or time off from school and a couple of potential colleges you've always wanted to see, (I suggest you stay local at first, so you can be efficient with time and money for the longer, more expensive trips). Then…

Go online or call if you need to. Yes, you can do that. You know that thing attached to your fingertips 24/7, is not a Snapchat or texting machine, it is actually a phone. Therefore, you can talk to people to find out if the schools you plan to visit have formal tours and information sessions available. If so register for the tours and go. See how it feels to you, take notes and pay attention to the student's actions and behavior while you are there. This is an important part of your college search experience and overall success in ultimately choosing which college you will attend after you are finished with your process. Therefore, please take the time to do it right. More on visits in the next section.

Make it a fun experience for all of you. Maybe find an interesting attraction or restaurant nearby so all of you know that no matter how the actual college visit goes there will be something fun to look forward to.

This will take the pressure off of everyone and enable you to go through the visit without getting complaints or disappointment expressed by the student.

See a big school, small school, public school, private school, city school and rural school at all different selectivity levels (in other words, don't just see the most competitive schools, see others because you will be surprised how amazing and competitive they are as well). This will enable the student to get a better understanding of the types of schools and environments they may like so you can be efficient later on.

You don't need to know your student's SAT or ACT scores or what their major is to start visiting schools. See them now (assuming your student is at least a high school sophomore) so they understand the differences, don't get as influenced by their friends and can start to see how this big, scary project can be done reasonably.

No matter where you are in the process the most important thing to do is start now! Everything you do and learn can only help you as you progress through the process. Manage your time efficiently, don't follow the paths of others and become educated on the colleges out there so you can make smart decisions going forward.

Russ' Rules... For Staying Cool

1. **Don't let the process overwhelm you.**

   Start now. Talk about college with each other. Get an idea what everyone wants and expects. Be open with the discussion and find opportunities to start the process sooner versus later so you don't increase the stress surrounding the process later on.

2. **Don't let the past limit your desire to take action**.

   Students mature at different times. They come into their social and academic primes at different times despite the effort they put in. Hard work is expected and appreciated but sometimes there are other factors that impact a student's ability to perform as best they can. It's never too late to change the trajectory that you are on. Colleges have done this before. They know that freshman year may have been tough for you. They know that standardized tests can cause havoc and not be an indicator of your ability to perform once you are at their school. What they look for mostly, is that you are improving year over year. Make solid progress. It's never too late to show that and put your best foot forward. Don't let your past define who you want to be and where you

   want to go.

3. **Start seeing colleges.**

Start close, see different types of schools, make the trip(s) fun and use them to start having needed conversation so you are all on the same page. Talk to people who are attending colleges you may be interested in. Gather as much information as possible so you become an informed college bound student and parent. To try to set the stage for your upcoming college journey I have shared two guides that I often hand out when I do presentations. Please read them and take them to heart. The process can seem complicated, but it doesn't need to be. Keeping a perspective that is reasonable for all involved can really help you along in many ways. I hope you enjoy and apply these "rules" throughout your voyage.

By Russ Vitale "The Cool College Guy"

The College Visits

"Make them Vertical, Not Just Horizontal."

Russ

Let's talk about some ways to fortify your process, give you better footing and get you on your way.

Usually when I suggest that students and families start college visits I get some pushback. They often think it is too soon and if they don't know their standardized test scores it is impossible to know where to go. As we discussed in the previous chapter this is not true according to the "Cool College Guy". But, how do you do a visit, so you get the most out of it? I will help you with that in a moment but before I do, here are some additional things families bring up as they consider if and when they should start visiting colleges.

There are three questions that I hear most often when parents and families are considering visiting;

How do we see schools when he or she doesn't know what they want to major in?

How do we see schools when we don't have the students SAT or ACT scores?

How do we see schools, when we don't know which type of school is going to be the best for our child?

Granted, these are great questions. However, they are not necessary when you want to visit a school or before you schedule visits. The student's scores may change, and yes, that will impact the student's ability to be considered for admission. But a visit is simply to get a feel of what a particular college offers and what the school feels like to the student. It would be nice if the student knows what his or her major was before applying for college, but 80% - 85% of the students across the country, will change their major at least once during their freshman year of college. There are majors that exist that they don't even know about yet. So, if this is the criteria a family uses to pick a college, it will already be obsolete by the end of the first or second semester of college, if it takes that long.

In my opinion it is most important to make sure that the school is a great academic, social, geographic, cultural, athletic (if it applies), and financial fit for the student and family.

When I say academic fit in this instance I don't actually mean based on career major. Instead I mean we want to make sure that the student is challenged, however not overwhelmed by the workload. Access to support when needed in the competitive nature that exists within the school is also important to ensure they are not overwhelmed which can lead to other potential pressure issues. Therefore, it is important to talk to students attending the school you visit to understand how they handle their workload, what access to help they have and if they are able to have a balanced experience. And this doesn't mean talking to or hearing what the tour guide says only, which we will address shortly.

When it comes to social, geographic and cultural fit, it is important that the culture of the college as well as the overall temperament of the student body matches yours. I always say that college is not a 4-year vacation for a student, it's a place to learn, be challenged and hopefully position oneself for a job upon graduation. Sounds nice right parents? However, it is important that a student feels comfortable with people like them because obviously the happier they are, the more likely they will be successful academically as well (if they don't take the social scene too far). So, it is important to talk to as many kids as possible, take in the social environment and make sure it fits your personality, learning style and overall desires.

Financial fit is one aspect that many families struggle with. If a school costs more, it doesn't mean it's better. You get that right? We have a tendency to think if it costs more it is better. That is not true with anything, but especially not with picking colleges. I always advise my families, so they have financial options. One school may be very expensive (many schools are $60,000+ these days) and I am pretty positive they won't get any money regardless of how great the student is academically. Another school may be the same price but offer merit money based upon those same academics. And another may have a lower sticker price, and maybe offer money as well. By providing these options to the families I work with it is then up to the family to make a decision as to what is the best school for them. But having these options is key rather than having every school cost $60,000 plus and no options that are more palatable from a financial perspective.

So, before we get into detail on what you should do, let's briefly share what most people do so we can clearly see the difference.

The Horizontal Visit

What most do but what you want to avoid at all costs!!!

When you actually start your college visits it's very important that a student actually give us their opinion of what they think about the school and their on-campus experience. But I can't tell you how many times when I ask a student what they thought of the school they say, "My tour guide was awful". If I had a dollar for every time I've heard these words when I asked the student this question, and the parents as well, what they thought of the school when they visited, my daughter's college tuition for one year would be paid and then some.

Over and over again I hear this and I nicely but directly let everyone know that this is the wrong criteria to use to judge a school that may be good for you and deserves your application later on. The tour guide is one person. You shouldn't judge a school from that alone. I understand that if the tour guide is exciting, interesting and funny it makes the whole experience much better. However, the tour guides are also kids. They can be nervous, stressed about exams, or even downright hung over, or worse they could be a Sociology major, Ugh! Just kidding there is nothing wrong with being a Sociology major, obviously, but if you're interested in something else other than Sociology and they know little about the Occupational Therapy program or any other program that you might be interested in, that could leave you dissatisfied. That doesn't mean the school is a bad school.

It just means that your tour guide is not informed and educated as they need to be.

Also, many families give priority to the tour and ignore the Information Session. Please do not do this!! **The Information Session** is key, though maybe not as exciting for some of you. We will discuss that more but DO NOT JUST DO THE TOUR and go home.

Last, I hear all the time that the weather didn't cooperate when a family visited a school. Really? I mean I get that no one wants to walk around in the rain or snow. However, as unfortunate as this is, weather is another one of those uncontrollable items that we shouldn't allow to impact our opinion on a school. If it rains every day and you don't want rain, we can address that. But weather happens all over. Don't make a decision on the appropriateness of a school based upon the weather when you were on campus.

A horizontal visit is what I think 99% of people do when they see colleges. They do a tour and make that the priority and maybe do an information session if it fits into their schedule. I think it should be the opposite way around. I've been on many college campuses and as much as I feel the tour is sometimes a waste of time, I'd do it to hear what an actual student has to say about their experience and see how prepared they are. Here's how it usually goes…

The student tells us what we will be seeing on the tour and gives us highlights of what to expect. Then without a doubt they say, "I'll be walking backwards so please let me know if I am about to bang into anything".

That's the big accomplishment and the focus for the whole tour. I understand it's not easy to walk backwards throughout all tours. With all the distractions, parents and students often do not ask any real questions. As I move to the front of the line, there is a 50/50 chance that I will get an answer. This is frustrating for me as well, but it is a necessary part of the process to gather information, so you can make the best college decision.

But let's continue. The rest of the horizontal visit consists of looking around to see if there are kids doing fun things, and maybe you grab a bite to eat so you can rate the food. Don't get me wrong I eat six or seven meals per day, so I understand the significance of food. However, most college food is fairly similar. There are exceptions of course but you can always find something that works. Then you go home and make a judgment on the superficial, high-level attributes and characteristics of the school that you just saw. Though it's better than nothing I suppose, it's not nearly as effective as it should be for most people

Tour guides, doing the tour only, weather, and food are what many people use as their primary criteria for keeping a school on their list or not. This is because most people don't really understand how to visit a school. So, without any further delay, let me introduce you to; The Vertical College Visit.

The Vertical College Visit

I talk to my students about how to do what I call The Vertical Visit rather than a Horizontal Visit. I have been on many informational sessions and tours, at many different colleges over the years. I can't tell you how many of these sessions I have attended where people feel like they are wasting time. It's almost as if they are saying

"Okay. We are here. We can check this off our list". There truly is no point visiting if you are not going to at least try to get the most out of it, wouldn't you agree?

Sometimes the visit will not provide what you need to make a decision. But some parents, just shake their head as if it is not important. Personally, even if this wasn't my career and passion I would not drive two hours with my daughter without making sure I get the information I need to help her decide how much she likes the school and if it may be a good fit for her.

And when families are there, the student is often bored out of their mind, exhausted from their crazy schedules, thinking about their friends and are not mentally prepared to understand how to evaluate a college. If this is the case, they obviously aren't ready to make a good decision about a school they are visiting. That's why the student should have a list of questions or a checklist with them as they listen to the information session and do the tour, so they can walk out of the visit with tangible criteria to help them evaluate the school properly.

The information sessions may seem boring at times but, many sessions are given either by admissions people or students who attend the school. Now I know some may be terrible public speakers and may not have the information or experience necessary to provide real content that you can write down and save as a solid reference point. This is unfortunate, but you should still listen closely so that you get valuable information regarding specific programs, the importance of early decision, social activities, etc.

Just to be clear.........

I know it's tough and often the student will make a judgment on the school depending on;

   Their personal state of mind at the time - for example; tired, happy, stressed, resistant, impatient.

The weather. If it's a nice sunny day where kids are outside playing Frisbee and having lively conversation, they love the school. If it's rainy and no one is around they think it's a boring place and may not be interested. "Next!"

Perception of whether the school is a good school based upon their friend's opinions or some useless rating report they saw giving them the idea that the school you are visiting is a "safety" for them.

But – none of these issues should be used to evaluate the school or to make a decision. Like I said– some schools may look better on a sunny day but there is no guarantee that the weather makes it a better place and it's going to eventually rain so don't let that influence your decisions. If the school is in a cold climate, seeing the school in the summer is not a good idea. See what I mean? The whole point is to find the right school with the right benefits and see the school as it really is and will be. Visiting a school with an open mind enforces the *bridge to the best of life concept*. Too much analysis can hinder the decision, but too swift of a decision based upon insignificant criteria could be the wrong way to go about it as well.

About the winter school; I understand that going in the summer might be when you have time to see the school and that's fine. However, before you make a decision to go and attend that school, it is a very good idea to go in the height of winter to understand what it's like there when you may be attending. You will need to be ready to tolerate the low temps! These decisions are part of the dynamic process of choosing the right college.

So, The Vertical College Visit looks like this...

- Contacting admissions prior to your visit to see if there are options to attend a class, meet a professor in a given department, get information on specific majors and programs, meet with a coach, etc.

- Doing some research about the school prior to your visit so you're familiar and can ask next level questions while on-campus. Be sure to ask questions on many topics and angles based on your personal preferences or curiosities.

- Bringing a list of questions to get specific answers while you're on campus so you have a long list of pros and cons to look at when you return from the visit.

- Sitting in the cafeteria or student center to watch the interaction of students. See what they're talking about and get an idea of the social scene as well as the academic pressure that exists at the school.

Now when you look at the students, what are you looking for? As an example, are the students sitting separately (alone) or are they in groups? If they are in groups that might mean that there's a healthy social situation at the school. You will need to be alert to the social interaction experience when you walk the halls, so be prepared now.

Even when they're in a group they may be talking about a project they're working on, the party they went to last night, a sporting event they attended, or something relative to the academic demands of the school. All of these can be helpful, so you get some indication of the balance between work and fun that exists there.

If many students seem to be sitting alone, it could mean that the school is has a very competitive academic environment where nobody wants to give information to their competition (classmates). If this is the case, you have to be able to tolerate impersonal interaction or understand that you may need to work a little harder to break the ice, so you can find your friend group.

Both scenarios could be an indication of what the social scene may be like and therefore one might be more conducive to your student's happiness than another. That is why doing informal tours on your own and talking to students who are currently attending is so important.

So, ask questions of students – not just the tour guides - to get a real feel for how campus life and academics are at the college. This is especially true if you are from out-of-state. I always emphasize the need to talk to other out-of-state students as much as possible when visiting a state school. It is important everywhere, so you understand the warmth, or lack thereof due to geographical and cultural differences. But if you are considering a state school this means that there will typically be many in-state students attending (duh, right?). Well of course these in-state students may love the college. They are with the same group they have been with since middle school or earlier. Their friend groups are already established but you will need to find yours. This will be a very different experience for you if you are out-of-state and you need to understand how that might go.

Here are some additional ideas on how to do a deeper dive into your Vertical Visit.

- Of course, you can see the dorms and classrooms but understand what the average class sizes are and if you will have access to the professors if you need help. If not, what kind of support is provided and how accessible is it?
- Meet with the Career Center so you understand the probabilities of getting an internship, what the process is, how many students

get an internship that the college helps them with (as opposed to those the student gets for themselves without any help from their college) as well as what percent of students go to graduate school, have jobs by major, etc.

- Meet with a professor and/or students in a program you are considering. Find out the potential for research opportunities, how they teach (practical or theoretical or both), how competitive it is and how demanding the curriculum is for that specific program.

- Meet with a coach if you think you want to and can play a sport at the college. Ask pointed questions to assess whether or not they are truly interested and if you would potentially have a spot on their team.

- Ask the Admissions Office for the admissions contact for your high school. Many, not all, colleges have representatives in admissions responsible for applicants from your school. They serve as a great resource to get additional information as well as to review your application upon you applying. It is important to meet with them and that they know who you are. Many schools are flooded with applications these days. It is important that the admissions person responsible for your school knows who you are and that you are seriously interested in their school.

- Meet with the Financial Aid Office if finances are important to you and your family. Sit down with them to understand their process and the potential for you to qualify for both merit and need based aid. Just like buying a car, house or business, it is important to understand the process and if a school is in your budget before you get too far along the process. Too many people don't do this because they don't want to disappoint their child or because they think it could negatively impact the admission decision. The first is a family thing but all I will say is that the disappointment will be much greater should your child be accepted and then you need to tell them it's not in your budget. Second, to be clear, you doing your financial homework will absolutely not impact your student's admission decision. Therefore, if finance is something you need to consider, ask questions, meet with people so you can become educated on the financial aid process for that specific college.

- Assess the geographic impact of a school. This is important enough to mention twice. As I said many kids at state schools have gone to elementary school, middle school and high school together. They already, therefore, have a group of friends and cliques as soon as they walk on campus. This is essentially 13th – 14th – 15th – 16th grade for them. So of course, they like it and that's great for them. But out-of-state students have to find their new friends and cliques. Talk to as many out-of-state students as possible because you'll be most likely faced with many of the same challenges they had if you attend the school in the future. Transition is not easy for everyone. Find out what yours may be like including informally, and formally, such as your ability to join activities, fraternities/sororities, and clubs. Some schools have an application process even for clubs, so it is important to know this, so you can manage your social expectations while on campus.

- Take notes and take 10 to 15 minutes listing your first impressions, opinions of the school as well as things you still would like to find out in the future. This will help you keep track and be a reference later to jar your memory, and maybe even to be used for essay writing on your application.

Russ' Rules... For Staying Cool

1. **Schedule a college visit but do more than just the campus tour.**

   You can schedule a visit usually online but look for tours that might specialize in a certain academic area such as engineering or physical therapy if your student has those interests. Call Admissions to see if you can sit in on a class or meet the head of a department so you can really find out about the school and its teaching philosophy which may differ by department. Do a thorough visit.

2. **Don't judge the appropriateness of a school based upon superficial criteria.**

   Things such as the ability of your tour guide and weather should be good for general conversation but not to make a lasting decision on whether or not the school is a good fit for you. Do a thorough tour so you get a real feel for what the school offers and if it is a good match for you academically, socially and otherwise. Talk to as many students as possible, observe them on campus (not in a creepy way, just to see how they interact and to get a good idea of the social vibe) and attend activities or events if possible.

3. **Document your visit so you can use the notes you took in the future when you are finalizing your college list.**

> Take 10 to 15 minutes to write down what you liked about the school, who you met and what you learned. Also, write down what you didn't like and things that you would like to find out either if you visit again or if you speak with people who attend the college. These notes will help keep everything organized for later reference and maybe even for your college application process as well.

By Russ Vitale "The Cool College Guy"

64 | P a g e

You Are What You Test...
Or Are You?

*"Testing is important, but don't let your
results consume or define you."*

Russ

Standardized testing is a necessary evil when it comes to the college process. Yes, there are 800+ schools that are SAT and ACT optional and you can go to www.fairtest.org for the latest complete list. However, this obviously limits the types of schools and choices for the student to apply to because not all schools have an optional testing policy. To have more options for the student it is recommended that the student find out which test is best for them (ACT or SAT), or which test they hate least, as I say to my clients.

Let's face it, it's true that if given the choice of playing sports, hanging out at Starbucks, going to the mall or 100 other more fun things to do, I'm sure you would not like to take an ACT or SAT instead. I mean it probably ranks right there with cleaning your room and I get it. I tell my students that if they like taking these tests then I'd like to have them go see a psychologist to find out what's wrong with them. For most students they aren't fun.

So, there are several things you can do to make this ominous and potentially complicated endeavor mush less so.

The first questions you'll face are:

- Which tests do you take?

- When do you take them?

- When do you prepare?

- How do you prepare?

- How many times do you need to take them?

Whew, that's a mouthful.

Let's break it down so you have clarity and a plan.

The student should take the test that they will do best on. It's as simple as that.

It doesn't matter if it's the ACT or SAT. This is very different from when I went to school. Growing up in New York everyone took the SAT. No one talked about and most people didn't even know there was an ACT. This has completely changed over the years and as a matter of fact despite what data you may see, the ACT has actually eclipsed the SAT as far as the number of tests administered over a majority of the last 5 to 7 years.

Both tests have gone through some changes and they are more similar now in content and scoring (as of 2018) than they've ever been (see the chart comparing these tests at the end of this section). Since they are more similar, certain testing techniques and principles may be interchangeable from a preparation perspective.

However, as the chart lists, there are some major differences between them and we will address a couple of those differences shortly.

The math level that the student is (in while in high school) can impact greatly the timing of when a student should take a test.

The earlier Algebra 1, Algebra 2 and Geometry are taken, the more prepared the student will be to take the math portion of either test. A student taking Pre-calculus their junior year should be ready to take the test earlier in their junior year if it fits better into their schedule and they have prepared adequately for it. A student in Algebra 2 junior year will be more likely to take a test in February or later to ensure they have the math necessary to answer as many questions as possible.

There are exceptions to every rule and this is not meant to be a specific instruction manual on testing strategies. However, these guidelines can happily put your mind at ease relative to timing, which is a big concern for most students and parents. Remember, other than money your most valuable asset is time and we need to be efficient with it. By the way, none of these guidelines will put you behind from the college application process even for early decision.

Often times I am asked by parents if their student will be at a disadvantage by testing later in their school year. I absolutely understand this concern and if it makes you feel any better, my own daughter will be taking Algebra 2 junior year and will be on this same schedule. Therefore, you can rest easy and understand it is more important to have the student test at the time that they are best prepared for rather than to have them take a test early and not do as well for many reasons.

How many times a student should test is dependent upon how well a student does, obviously.

In general, it should be expected that the student take two tests in the winter or spring of their junior year and one test in the fall of their senior year. This does depend greatly though on how they perform, the colleges they are interested in and if there is any consideration for acceptance into an Honors program or for consideration for merit money.

I'd like to be crystal clear on a myth I am asked about pretty regularly. I believe it is a complete myth that certain tests are easier than others. I have never found that to be true. One trend I have seen though is that when students struggle, or don't do as well as they wanted when they take the test earlier on, often times if they do improve, their best results are typically in the fall of their senior year.

Call it maturity, panic, last chance luck, or whatever you like, but I have seen this happen more often than not. I suppose we can say that means it is a potential trend, but I don't think it is related to one SAT or ACT being easier than another. I attribute this more to student preparation and focus.

"I just wanted to take the test to see what it's like". "His/Her results don't really matter right?"

I hear this all the time. As I have said, there's no one right way to do anything in life. But, there is a more effective and efficient way to handle this part of the process especially if your student tends to be an over thinker. This is common with lots of kids who have the "weight of the world" on them to perform well, or think they do. This is usually self-imposed where they feel their college dreams are all over if they don't get a certain score the first time.

You and I know this is not really true, but this is what they convince themselves is factual. I found this especially true with my athletes and students who are used to performing well in school. They typically are more likely to think about everything to obsessive levels at times and take a test before they are properly prepared which can do tremendous damage to their psychological well-being going forward. Therefore, I always suggest that students delay the test to a date that is optimal for them, so they can do the proper preparation rather than take a test before they are truly ready.

Let me share an analogy that may resonate with some of you.

Now, I have run two marathons. Yeah, not sure what I was thinking? But I did. If you are a runner, and you have run a marathon or needed to train for any event, you understand there's a lot of preparation that goes into it. For training purposes, you need to pace yourself for mile 6, mile 14, mile 22, and so on so you can finish. Someone in the right physical and emotional mindset can finish the event as strong as they can if they trained properly and learned how to pace themselves. (Notice I didn't say race, I said pace. When I ran my marathons, I did not see them as races either. I mean who am I kidding? I wasn't beating any speed records. I just wanted to finish with the best time I could without injury).

The testing process in my opinion is very similar. If you try to run without building the foundation through training, miles and miles of training, you're not going to make it to the end, and if you do, you are most likely not going to do it well. Testing is the same. Students need the right foundational work, so they are prepared to do as well as they can.

If not, yes, they can take the test again, multiple times even, but if they have in their head that they are "bad test takers", now for every future test they take this nasty thought can be in the back of their mind. It's something that may always exist or present itself strongly depending upon the student. The damage done by being unprepared can be irreparable.

Therefore, I'm a big believer when it comes to major impact life events (testing in this case but other life events as well) that you approach it with a plan, take action but also know the timing of your action is just as important as taking action in the first place. For some students taking standardized tests is an academic and mental marathon. Proper preparation and timing is key to helping them be in the best position to perform well.

With this in mind, let's give you some additional tips for timing and planning purposes;

If your student is in AP courses sophomore year or advanced math, meaning Pre-calculus or higher, it is possible that they can take a Math or SAT Subject Test* for the correlating AP courses they are in. This test is different from the SAT or ACT and is required by some of the more selective colleges.

The timing of when a student may consider taking these tests will most likely be in May of their sophomore year. It is not critical to take them in the student's sophomore year, but it can help lighten their load for junior year if they do. As I said, Subject Tests are required or recommended by some college(s) that your student wants to apply to. In my opinion, when it says "recommended" or "optional" it always means it's required especially if the school is highly selective.

Another reason to take a Subject Test is to show proficiency in a given subject and to provide additional academic proof of a student's ability to excel in a specific area.

When the Subject Test is taken, I advise my students to not rely solely on the teacher's AP test preparation because some teachers are better than others at preparing their students for the AP exams. There may be a small yet significant difference between a Subject Test and the correlating AP test depending on the specific subject. (By the way, to utilize the tests you take to strengthen your admission positioning the student absolutely needs to do well on their score. A score of at least 700 out of 800 or greater is preferred).

In order to do that I always suggest that in February or March before they plan to take the test that they buy a book and they take multiple exams. This will help them determine whether or not tutoring is something they need before they take the actual test. It is an extra step, but it is necessary to ensure the student is properly prepared and will perform well.

*I know we haven't spent a lot of time discussing Subject Tests. As I said, these are tests that some highly selective schools require or recommend are submitted as part of the admission process. There are Subject Tests in Math (Math 1 & 2), Biology, Chemistry, Physics, U.S. History, English Literature as well as others.

These tests are typically a much deeper dive into the material learned in the subject and should have some similarities with the corresponding AP exams. That is why I stated that it is usually best that a student is in an AP class when considering taking the corresponding subject test.

However, students can always do additional work (crazy I know) to properly prepare if they are not in an AP level class. In addition, I always suggest that a student who is considering taking a Subject Test buy a book and take at least 3 practice exams to see how they do and to gauge if additional work, material and/or tutoring is needed.

Because these tests are usually submitted to highly selective schools and because you are taking them to show strong proficiency in that subject, I usually advise my students that anything under 700 out of 800 is not really going to help their case for admission in most cases.

This is not a rule. It is an observation from advising many students over the years.

*If your student is completing Algebra 2 or greater in their current year math course they should take a simulated SAT **and** ACT (but not in the same week because, let's face it, that's just mean).*

After their final exams, but before July 4 is when I usually suggest students do this and this will be most likely in their junior year. However, again, if they've taken Algebra 2 and finish it after sophomore year you can always do the simulated tests at that point instead. I say that it's important to take these simulated tests after final exams because obviously students should be focused on and make sure that their GPA is the best it can be with no distractions. I also suggest that you take these simulated tests before July 4 because after July 4 most kids, and most people, go into summer mode.

In my opinion you don't need to have the student prepare for this beta-test and honestly, they shouldn't. However, you do want them engaged from an academic perspective and you want them still in "school mode" so they will do as best they can and focus on giving their best effort. After July 4 I find most students tend to be in big time summer mode, laid-back, thinking about the beach, spending time with their friends, maybe starting a job, whatever they will be doing in the upcoming summer. The bottom-line is they are definitely not thinking about taking another test once summer freedom kicks in.

The goal of taking the simulated tests is not necessarily to maximize their score. Shocking I know because it's all about the score, right? Not really. But please take back that gasp and understand what I'm trying to say here.

The point of taking a simulated test, both the ACT and SAT, is more to see which test is a better fit for the student as far as timing and content so you can put a testing plan in motion.

I always tell my clients, "You don't come to me to be wrong and you don't come to me to be late". In my opinion this process will certainly avoid the being late factor and hopefully with some analysis and discussion by qualified people in the standardized testing field, it will help you to find the right test, so you can create a plan for how to proceed in the student's junior year.

If by chance the student tests very well on the SAT, then there may also be consideration for some prep before the PSAT in October of their junior year. The purpose of this is to try to have them qualify for National Merit which is a distinction appreciated by highly selective schools.

If you follow the advice above, you are most likely ahead of most people you know. This is great for you planners out there. But let's now discuss what most people do so you can feel even better about your new course of action.

The Typical Testing Experience

In most cases a junior takes the PSAT in October and gets their results that December, two months later. Already you can see that if you listen to me, you started in June of sophomore year.

Doing what most people do just lost you seven months of the college process or approximately 39% of your planning time. This is considerable as you can see. As I've said before and I continue to repeat to my clients as we go through the process, "Other than money, the most vital asset to any family or student is **TIME!**" Waiting seven months and starting seven months later can really cause lots of additional stress and anxiety for the family and for the student that is unnecessary.

Just to make sure that the point is obvious, if I asked you to give me $39 for every hundred dollars you had or earned, how would that feel? I'm guessing that wouldn't feel so good. I know I wouldn't be happy about that. So again 39% of your planning time lost. (Lost time of visiting colleges because many feel they have to wait until they get scores to start visiting schools which you already know is not the case.)

There is often lost time in planning and preparing for the standardized tests that need to be taken which may be critical to the net outcome for the student and the family, in their senior year).

OK so let's return to what most students do after they get their PSAT results in December of their junior year. They then sign up for a spring test which is typically the SAT and realize that they haven't done anything to really prepare, and they also by the way ignore the ACT completely as an option.

Even if the ACT may be a better test for the student by not taking the simulated test, and doing what most people do, you could have your student not reaching their full potential which may impact their acceptance and potential for merit money down the road. Furthermore, by ignoring this other test as a possibility you also may have wasted time and money but also you may be increasing the frustration for the student if they are trying to take a test that isn't right for them.

There may be options available and maybe even a different level of school(s) that the student can consider if the results end up being much greater on the ACT than the SAT. Now in many cases I have found that the differences between the scores are fairly minimal to start. It is usually about timing and comfort with the test content and format. However, for some students because of the way the tests are structure and the timing there may be big differences in the score. It is important to know that by taking that extra step (taking the simulated tests) you don't make this huge mistake!

Of course, there are many different routes the student can take to optimize their test scores, and I'm not trying to say it's my way or you'll not get where you want to be. However, if you want to maximize the student's potential and options, as well as minimize the stress related to testing and the overall college process, The Cool College Guy's method will be a significant help. It will help lower the stress and anxiety plus you'll have a plan.

All of these things will put you in a better position to optimize results and make you aware of the various options available for your student and family.

Switching gears, to the nonacademic perspective of standardized testing, there are a lot of things to consider. I always emphasize that these tests are academic but are also very mentally challenging as well. As mentioned prior, a student needs to be prepared properly and if they're stuck thinking that they are "bad test takers" meaning they are now doomed to go to a terrible college as a result, the lasting effect could be quite significant.

We want to avoid this at all costs. Therefore, in an attempt to make the potentially complicated easier, it is critical to manage expectations of parents and students so there is very minimal panic (if any). That way the student can focus on what they need to do as far as prep rather than create more anxiety or test paralysis.

Keep the testing results in perspective please.

No one cares what you got on the test!! Okay other than your parents, you, and the colleges you submit your scores to. But other than that, no one else cares what you got on these tests.

Your friends do not care what you got. So why do they ask you say? It's because they want to know if you are competition for them. It's really all about them and has nothing to do with you. Don't get me wrong, this does not mean that you have lousy friends or that your friends don't care about you. But your friends are feeling a lot of the same anxiety and stress that you are, and they want some of the same things.

And your friends want to know who they need to worry about taking their spot at a given school if they apply to the same school as you. For this reason, as well as about 20 others, there's no reason to post your scores on Facebook or Snapchat to let everyone know what you got. Now again, I'm not looking to tell you that you should or shouldn't do this. But to me, that just raises the anxiety for everybody.

It also raises the competition level to an unnecessary level when most people think it was there already. You don't need to tell everyone what you got. It is your business and your business alone. You do not need to play that game if you don't want to.

Also, once you get into college, no one cares what you got on your ACT or SAT. I have to tell you even the business that I'm in, where I talk about ACT's and SATs all day long, no one has ever asked me when I got on the SAT. Okay that's not totally true, my daughter asked me and there may have been a couple of other people and of course I was honest with them. But after you graduate college your potential employer won't ask, your friends won't ask unless they are at a party and getting silly and have nothing else to talk about, and your employees, coworkers and your clients won't ask either.

So, can you believe that this thing that you have spent a year or more worrying about and are using to define your self- worth will be obsolete and a useless piece of data once you start to go to college and beyond? Can you see how things change?

So, if that's the case, do the best you can to prepare, have a plan and optimize your score so you have the options you want. Then, after you take the tests, accept the scores and use them to find colleges that are awesome for you. As we discussed there are many great colleges out there if you're open-minded and flexible beyond the bumper sticker pride. I'm spending time on this because I believe it's very important and I see it day in and day out.

The pressure that kids put on themselves relative to their standardized test scores is amazing and certainly takes a toll on them. Yes, they are set on their own goals. Yes, they want to do as well as they can in most cases. However, they're more concerned (most of the time) about two things:

First, their comparison to others as they worry what other's results are and if they are smarter than they are. They are also concerned that if they don't do well on a standardized test or obtain a certain score, it will significantly minimize their potential to get into their top choice school and they will be doomed forever. It is true that the highly selective schools do expect and do want high ACT and SAT scores.

Therefore, the higher your test scores are the better chance you will have for serious admission consideration. But getting these higher scores is no guarantee either. So, I say again, do the best you can to prepare, have a plan as we just laid out but please do not stress. Don't think that life is going to be so much more challenging for you if you don't get a certain score on the test.

And another thing, when you go to your high school reunion 5, 10, 20, 30 years later, the people that you remember being great students, with great SAT or ACT scores are just as likely as you (or anyone else) to be successful or unsuccessful, happy or unhappy. There is no known correlation that I'm aware of that says if you have higher ACT or SAT score that your success and happy quotient is something that will be much greater as compared to everyone else.

See the testing process for what it is. It is a necessary criterion for college consideration. But I don't let it define my students and I don't think you should either. Your standardized test score is not who you are! It's one test or as I've said, maybe two or three or more tests that you have taken in a given time. The point is that it's a minuscule part of your whole life and who you are.

After you apply to schools, get into college and start your college journey, please don't dwell on your scores because no one else will. Don't give the scores the power to determine your happiness or success potential. It's very hard to accept this as all of your friends and all the people you're talking to keep asking you about your scores.

I get that. But as obsessed and entrenched as you are in it right now, after you apply and get accepted to the colleges that you apply to, it will not matter. It will not define you and it will not impact your future success or happiness in college, your academic performance (despite what some supposed studies may insinuate), your financial success, or your personal and social life.

Russ' Rules… For Staying Cool

1. **The testing process is just that, a process.**

   Don't look at your PSAT results or first simulated test results and doom yourself to less than what you want to achieve. It takes time and practice to be the best you can be regarding testing in most cases. Start early, create a plan and implement the plan so you can optimize your results and be as productive as possible throughout your college application and admission journey

2. **Identify which test is best for you.**

   Colleges in my experience don't care which test you take and submit for admission consideration. Therefore, take both as practice test to determine which fits your learning and academic style best. Then pick the test dates that work best for you given your school and activity schedules. Once you choose the dates prepare the way you need to, so you ensure, come test day, that you are ready to present the best you to achieve the best results possible. Also, don't forget Subject Tests if they are required by the colleges you are considering.

3. **Don't let test results define you.**

As we discussed testing is a necessary evil. The better you do the better your chances for admission at the schools you are considering as long as all other criteria are within reason as well. However, the test scores do not guarantee you anything and they do not define you as far as your potential for success in college and beyond. As with everything is life, do the best you can, give it everything you have so there are no regrets when all is said and done. But once you are done go forward and make the best of every opportunity you have because that is where the true success and happiness comes from. Not from one test day in the spring or fall of your high school career.

Good luck!!

COLLEGE: Making the Complicated Easy

SAT vs ACT

What's The Difference?

Test Purpose	Designed to Measure acedemic achivement in: • Reading • Mathematics • English • Writing (optional) • Science	Designed to Measure: • Reading • Mathematics • Writing and Language • The SAT Essay (Optional)
Accepted for University Admission	The ACT is accepted by all colleges and universities in the United States and more than 225 other universities around the world.	Accepted by all US colleges.
Method of Scoring	Scores based on number of right answers. No penalty for incorrect answers.	Scores based on number of right answers. No penalty for incorrect answers.

CONTINUED ON THE NEXT PAGE

Information From the official ACT Website.[ii]

83 | P a g e

Test Content: 	**ACT Mathematics Test (60 items, 60 minutes)** Multiple-Choice 100% • Preparing for higher math • Number & Quantity • Algebra -• Functions • Geometry • Statistics & Probability • Integrating essential skills • Modeling **ACT Reading Test (40 items, 35 minutes)** Multiple-Choice 100% • Key ideas and details • Craft and structure • Integration of knowledge and ideas **ACT English Test (75 items, 45 minutes)** Multiple-Choice 100% • Production of Writing • Topic Development • Organization, Unity, and Cohesion • Knowledge of Language • Conventions of Standard English • Sentence Structure and FormationP • Punctuation • Usage **ACT Science Test (40 items, 35 minutes)** Multiple-Choice 100% • Interpretation of data • Scientific investigation • Evaluation of Models, inferences, and experimental results • Passage Formats on the Science Test: • Data Representation • Research Summaries • Conflicting Viewpoints **ACT Writing Test (optional) (1 prompt 40 minutes)** Measures writing skills emphasized in high school English classes and in entry-level college composition courses. Consists of one 40-minute essay.

Test Content: 	**SAT Mathematics (Total 58 items, 80 minutes)** • Calculator Portion (38 items, 55 Minutes) • Multiple-Choice 79%, Grid-In 21% • Heart of Algebra • Problem Solving and Data Analysis • Passport to Advanced Math • Other Topics *No-Calculator Portion (20 items with 25 minutes)* *Multiple-Choice 75%, Grid-In 25%* • Heart of Algebra • Passport to Advanced Math • Other Topics **SAT Evidence-Based Reading and Writing** Reading Test (52 items, 65 minutes) • US and World Literature • History/Social Studies • Science *Writing and Language Test (44 items, 35 Minutes)* • Careers • History/Social Studies • Humanities • Science **No Science Test** Note: Reading subject test is constructed of 40% science and the Writing and Language subject test is constructed of 25% science. **SAT Essay (optional) (1 task, 50 minutes)** Tests reading, analysis, and writing skills; students produce a written analysis of a provided source text.

By Russ Vitale "The Cool College Guy"

Majors, And How I Became "The Cool College Guy"

"It helps me in the kitchen but has nothing to do with how I make a living"

\- Russ

Who is the "Cool College Guy" and, how did I get here?

I grew up being told that I needed to find a job in a big company where I would have stability. I think this mostly came from my mother who was tired of living with financial stress and uncertainty. Back then (I'm not saying exactly how long ago it was, but it was when basketball shorts were a little shorter than they are today, how's that?), I saw people retiring from large companies. Most of them after many years of service, had at least some financial stability as a result. This seemed very appealing to me, so I thought I might give it a try.

Desperate for financial comfort of any sort, I did end up with a job with a very large company at the time. That company is still around but it is not nearly as big or prosperous today. However, the way it happened for me was very non-traditional. My college did not help me, nor did my throwing tons of resumes out into the universe. I help my students find internships and jobs, but this book is not aimed to address those things. Yet, this is an important thing to share so please bear with me.

I mention this because many things in life don't go exactly as planned or expected but that is okay because that doesn't mean you are destined for failure. Sometimes when things go in an unexpected direction, it is actually better for you although it doesn't feel like it at the time. I will be addressing this concept in greater detail later on so let's get back to the point.

I ended up playing on a softball team after college and overheard some teammates jabbing at each other. One guy in particular was making fun of the other five, calling them "losers" because they had interviewed with his brother at this large company and none of them got a job offer.

I asked why I hadn't had the opportunity to interview at the company, and after he stopped laughing and telling me that I had no chance, he agreed to connect us.

Well, long story short, they hired me, and I was there for 13 years before I voluntarily left.

At the time I thought I'd made it. I landed a job with a huge company and would be set for life! The first couple of years was torture, as I was put in a *churn and burn* sales position. I slowly became the elder statesman after lasting - and I do mean lasting- 2 1/2 years. Then I got a job at headquarters and despite moving around to different buildings within New Jersey, I had several more years of employment with this company.

In my new positions at the company headquarters I was lucky to travel the country to train and give presentations to salespeople on the products and services the company offered.

From this experience in corporate America, I found several of my passions and strengths - but was not able to fully pursue them during this time frame because of the demands of the job.

However, things are always subject to change, and the big corporate security setting became a stress and anxiety producing machine for many including me. Constant reorganizations and downsizings led to people being thankful that they still had a job despite the fact that they were working much more, taking on the responsibilities of those who were asked to leave, and had their pay and benefits dwindling each year. It was overall, a very hard time in my life and those of my co-workers.

Now I knew that the big corporate life was not for me if it was going to be like this. These massive, frequent changes solidified my decision that I needed to do something different. I started doing research and took some assessments to match my interests with potential careers. From my corporate experience I already knew I didn't want to be in a cubicle looking at a computer screen all day.

Nothing against that, but I knew I needed interpersonal interaction, movement and variety in order to stay active and to thrive. Plus, I wanted to help people. I was feeling that I myself hadn't received much, if any, help over the years to help me find my passion or to get pointed in a direction that appealed to me. I wanted to spare others of the same hardships and struggles I went through throughout my entire life (specific conversations about these difficulties may be shared another time, perhaps in another book).

Anyway, this won't be shocking given what I just shared but teaching came up over and over despite the fact that I didn't want to go back to school to become a teacher. I was frustrated and felt disappointed that in my thirties I was still unsure about what I wanted to do with my life. I wanted to know what I wanted to be when I grew up.

What's funny is how the universe sometimes presents things to you, and it's important that when those things show up - you are open and aware of them, even if you end up not pursuing them. I found you can always learn from them.

After lots of research and conversation with a diverse set of people, I found my passion and niche. It wasn't easy, and there were times I would question myself of its viability. I kept thinking about the alternative; going back into the corporate environment where there was considerable instability and all my efforts would be going towards the pockets of other people that I was supporting, rather than working for myself and my clients.

There was no way I was going back there so I kept going, as tough as it was. Things started to come together. At least now I knew I would be doing things for my clients, adding tremendous value, helping people with one of the most significant, stressful, uncertain and expensive milestones of the life and doing it for me!

I am sharing this with you because though my story is most likely not the way it will go for all of you, there is a chance you may find that your journey has some similarities. In today's world, fewer people seem to be in one company their whole lives.

It is likely that you may change company and career at least three times, so you need to know how to navigate the process as well as what to do when that change happens. This is a topic we may explore in another book, but the lessons are still very relevant and transferable to the college process in attempt to make things easy.

I wasn't clear from the beginning regarding what I wanted to do as far as my career and profession. In addition, the road I had taken to get where I was certainly wasn't direct or expected. Such is life, right? Again, we have to expect that all the life dynamics that others face and manage as they go through various life milestones will impact you as well in the college process and when you proceed through your life's goals and milestones. So, I would like to use this uncertain journey as a good introduction to the topic of picking a major and potential career.

Many parents ask me if they need to know what their child wants to do, study or be before they look at colleges. Though that may seem logical, that isn't necessary at all. We discussed that in the section on college visits. It obviously is something that students should think about but not necessarily use as the key driver to start to visit colleges. This is due to the fact that so many students change their major so many times while in college. Academic, social and financial fit are more important in my opinion, but let's get back to choosing a career.

I would venture a guess that you probably know what you don't want to do or areas of study which will be more difficult for you than others. This sounds backwards but it is how I approach the subject with my students. Process of elimination can lead us to potential. For example, if you're not much of a math or science person, Engineering and Actuary Science are probably not for you. It may not always be as obvious as this but there are career characteristics and responsibilities that you can assess to help you decide if they make sense for you, or not.

Likewise, if you don't want to sit in a cubicle and stare at a computer screen all day, Computer Science may not - emphasis on "may not" - be the right choice for you as a career. Given these examples, then how do you choose a major?

Most schools do ask you what your first and second choice for a major is and/or the school or college you will be applying to. For example, you may be applying to the School of Business at XYZ University. Yes, you also may have to choose your major but if you change your major in that same school, usually there's no difficulty or challenge in doing so. Therefore, changing from Marketing to Business Management is most likely a change that you can make quite easily. However, there may be some potential impacts on your admission decision based upon the major you choose or the school you decide to apply to within the college or university you are interested in.

Let me share an example. At some schools a Physical Therapy program or Business Management major might make it more difficult to get admitted to the school because of the more rigorous requirements for admission consideration, the smaller size of the program in general, or popularity of the major.

You should discuss this more as a family because it does have the potential to impact the student's interest in a major or school as well as their chances for admission on some level. (Remember, when we explained the Vertical Visit? That would be a great example of a key data point you need to ask the admissions contact about, so you understand the dynamics at that specific college. Just a suggestion).

The major a student is considering or is forced to choose as part of the application process (though it may not be a key driver as I said) is something you obviously can't ignore. What I recommend all my students do is take some kind of major and career assessment, so they can investigate different careers that match their interests, personality, values and skills. Granted, at 15 to 18 years old the skills and values are nowhere near fully developed.

Therefore, I put much more emphasis on interests and personality matching when I work with my students. This too can vary as a student develops and matures, however, it is the most accurate identifier at this young age in my opinion.

Let's face it, someone terrible with numbers isn't likely to love them and become an expert later on. To ensure that the college process goes easily, understanding these types of things can not only help give the student an idea what they may want to major in while in college, but it also can help identify the college environment that may be best for them.

In a different example, if a student is great with organization and details, matching these attributes to careers and majors with similar requirements obviously makes sense. Learning about these majors and which colleges offer them is important because that will obviously drive how your college list is developed.

I would like to point out that it is also important to know that there are majors offered in most colleges that we (all of us) don't even know exist at this point. Years ago, I don't recall knowing about a major called *Supply Chain Management* and *Health Informatics*. I mean it may have existed, but I don't recall knowing about it or anyone who actually had the major when I was growing up. Now many of my students share majors with me that I have often never heard of. I guess this is to be expected as we prepare for the new, fast changing world we live in.

Finding a major through your college experience that fits your interests and abilities is imperative in my opinion, so you build awareness of your strengths and likes as well as how to turn them into a potential career. But, depending on the source, I have seen data that states that anywhere between 70 -85% of college freshmen change their major at least once by the end of their freshman year of college.

That is OK, and you should know that there is a great possibility that will happen at some point for most of you. I know many of my students when I see them after they've already started college or after they graduated college, most of them have majors that we've never discussed and that are new to them. Some may even have jobs that differ from their major, like I do.

So, the point is, doing research to understand what your potential major may be can be helpful and it is something I suggest my students do as part of my process. However, using that as a main factor in finding schools, visiting schools and applying to schools may be a bit much, since so many students end up changing their major or finding something completely new once they attend college.

Try to think about possible majors, talk about them and do some research, but think of it more as a tactical consideration regarding the college admissions process.

To make my point, do you know anyone who thought they were going to major in one thing and changed their minds? I do. Just this college season (Fall 2018) a former client of mine started her freshman year and has already changed her major twice. Parents, do you know anyone who majored in ABC and now has a job doing something that isn't related to their major at all? I do. I know many. Me for example.

I believe I mentioned this before but I'm a Hotel/Restaurant major. The quote at the beginning of this chapter is something I tell everyone; "It helps me in the kitchen but has nothing to do with how I make a living" (directly at least). However, it absolutely taught me a lot about entrepreneurship and now I have my own business. I originally thought I was going to be an Accounting major until I took my first accounting class and realized very quickly it wasn't for me.

I am the perfect example of what I described above, and I'd like to think I turned our pretty good, so the same is possible for all of you.

Regarding my former students, usually this is not a surprise to me knowing what I thought about them as well as knowing the fact that most students do not have enough experience or know enough about themselves to be able to identify what is a good major for them going into college. Therefore, I really believe it is very unfair to put a student in that position and, often times, I find *a parent making this decision* for the student which is a whole different conversation. I understand why colleges ask, so they can manage their enrollment, but I really think it is unfair to most students. (By the way many colleges and more every year seem to have techniques and classes for freshman that help them learn about potential majors.

These programs are great, and I think every college should offer this option. It helps the student gain clarity and awareness plus it helps the college, so the student is more likely to graduate in 4 years and have a positive experience.

Instead many seem to base their major or their child's major upon what they think is prestigious. They may have heard that a specific major "earns the most money" or read things pointing them in that direction. However, this often can hurt from an *admissions process perspective.*

As I said before, you may be putting a student in a more competitive application pool which makes it harder for them to get admitted by following this approach. This also often makes the student very stressed and uncomfortable because it's a major that they don't know anything about.

If you fast forward to the student's college experience, a parent may be wondering why their kid is not interested, at least at this time, in pursuing it or challenged in college and not doing as well as they expected. I don't have to tell you this can often create conflict within the family that I feel is avoidable and will likely be unnecessary because of the high potential that the major will change in college anyway.

Side note to parents: Please give your child room to make the right decision for them to be successful throughout their college experience. Sometimes the bumper sticker colleges are not the right ones, nor are the bumper sticker equivalent in majors or careers. Just sayin...

It is my opinion that career and major exploration are an important part of the college process despite the uncertainty the young adult faces. Finding an academic path that matches the student's personality and interests whether it is specific, like Accounting, or generic like Humanities or something in between; starts the student in the direction of learning, gaining exposure, reality checks and adaptation to find something that exists and/or that they can create, to follow a passion that is newly found.

And when it comes to education, I believe education is not just about testing and results. I believe education, especially at the college level and beyond, is about creating a fire that leads to a passion within an individual. Regardless of whether or not the student or person feels it's going to be a lucrative major they should pursue their passion because if they do they will be more successful in college and more likely to find ways to support themselves.

This has been my experience and as a result how I advise all my students. I have found this to be true in real life myself as well. If you have a passion and you follow that passion intelligently, apply business acumen, add common sense and research, you can create and find a job or career that matches your interests and your personality (as well as your skills and strengths).

Is it a tougher road to travel? Sometimes, yes. But if you are aware of your strengths and follow a passion that represents who you truly are (inside and out), not only are you lucky, but you will find a way to make money doing it and be happier as a result! OK, off my soap box for now, thank you for indulging me.

It is obvious I feel that fulfillment comes from doing such exploration, research and introspection which far outweighs ending up in a career that provides you with no joy or happiness. In fact, it actually can have the exact opposite effect on you, your future family, your kids and those around you. Talk to adults and you will find many are doing things that have nothing to do with what they studied in college. Many had no idea they would be in the industry they are now. Despite these facts, they are still probably successful and hopefully happy in every way.

Don't put pressure on the process thinking you need to know every detail, because in the college process, as in life, we all know a direct line from what you think you want to what you end up doing is very rare. It is the learning process along the way that makes us better in every way.

So, to summarize, to me, career and major exploration is important but not something that should be applied with pressure. It also needs to be understood that it can impact the admission process. Lastly, though I understand that college is a significant expense and certainty that the student will graduate and make money is important, but a student who is responsible and driven will find their way.

A student who may lack in that department at the moment may

not have found their passion. By allowing them to explore in the process and while at college, can be what makes the difference in their life. They can find their passion and what interests them, so they can have a positive college experience, graduate in a reasonable time and hopefully find a job as a result.

My end goal with my students is helping them understand they don't need to know everything now. Finding their passion takes some time. It took me until I was 35. Pursuing your passion, doing something that brings you joy and happiness, and that enables you to sustain yourself, is what life should be about in my opinion. We all know the *happier we are, the more receptive we are to opportunities* when they are presented to us, and we even create them for ourselves and others which is truly amazing.

Russ' Rules... For Staying Cool

1. **Realize that life and the college process is not a straight line.**

    We all know that our journey from where we were, to where we are, to where we will be, can be filled with detours, road bumps and maybe roadblocks. It is important to learn from these deviations, embrace the new direction you are taking and continue FORWARD. Being flexible with our expectations and timelines is important. This doesn't mean you can't be highly motivated, you can. But don't be too rigid forcing something that isn't working. Don't get ahead of yourself projecting what you think may happen. Don't let potential derailments send you off course for too long. See them as new opportunities.

2. **Major and Career Exploration is an important part of the college process but...**

    It's very important that a student do research to understand and learn more about potential careers and majors *before they apply and attend college.* I also feel it's important that while they are in college - and beforehand if they are ready for it – students need to have exposure to lots of different careers, majors, professions and people who work in those areas. This way they can understand not just what these people do, but how they got where they are. Doing so will help them manage their expectations and think more clearly

COLLEGE: Making the Complicated Easy

about what they may want to do, as well as identify other opportunities that are out there. It may also impact the admissibility of your student as they apply to college so be careful to choose wisely, not force the decision and understand the potential impact on the student's admissions process.

3. Be receptive to all opportunities and feedback.

As I said roadblocks and detours are inevitable. It's how we respond to those and how we end up moving forward to find and learn about new experiences, new opportunities, new careers, new majors that is important. These things will present us with an open door to a future that may be temporary or maybe very long-lasting. Find your passion, what motivates you, what impacts and helps others and what makes you happy.

Learn by talking with people and by utilizing the resources at the college you attend so you understand the path you need to be on to pursue it. Then, once you do find it, pursue it with *reckless abandonment* (OK not completely reckless, but with lots of effort and drive).

If you are fortunate enough to find your passion in college or beyond, you will be as successful as you are capable of being and you will work harder than you ever imagined but love every minute of it. I was fortunate to find this, but it happened after 35 years and people who know me know patience is not always my virtue. I hope you find yours. But if you haven't yet, know it is always possible, just stay the course, remain open to opportunities and don't pressure yourself unnecessarily.

Creating a Realistic College List

"The college list drives everything"

-Russ

I know this sounds obvious as you read it, but I state this fact at every presentation, workshop and consultation I do. Why? Because hardly anyone puts a list together with that concept in mind. Let me tell you what most people do.

First off, not to repeat myself but most people start way too late, so they go to what they feel is comfortable because they don't know how else to get started. Second, they get all enamored with the glamour of the process and they want to tell others they are starting to visit schools. This is mostly for confirmation that they are "doing the right thing" but it's also to get people's attention with names of the schools they plan to see.

So, they pick the schools everyone else is seeing, even if the chances of their student getting admitted is slim to none, and their chance of affording it is even less likely. This comes largely from kids driving the process, "I want to see this school" and mom and dad just say okay because they don't know what else to do. It also comes from parents not knowing enough about the colleges out there these days and well, let's be honest, the parents' desire to give their child what they want and to sound impressive when they talk with their friends.

So, what should you do? Let me start by explaining what I mean when I say the college list drives everything. The schools that are on the student's list obviously determine the potential for acceptance, but they also largely impact the following;

- Cost,

- Timing of applying, meaning early decision, early action, rolling admissions etc.,

- The essay workload.

Let's give another example of what most people do. Many people don't understand how the financial aid process works in the college application arena.

Despite it being important that they do, most families ignore this aspect and unfortunately face it when it's too late; after the student has been accepted and they didn't receive any money or not enough money. Now the family is in a quandary that could have been avoided if they had gone about it in the correct way from the beginning.

That's just one example. I could go on and on, but I would rather give you simple tips on how you can be smarter about the process and make the complicated easier. So, let's break down the components I listed above so you understand what you should do and how they can impact the process.

This way you can try to minimize the uncertainty and disappointment when applying to schools for you and your family. So, I will share what you should do, but also what you should try not to do as well. Let's start with things you shouldn't do, because they are very common mistakes and you may be faced with them now.

These three things are areas where most people make mistakes when it comes to putting a college list together.

1. You can't go by online numbers or Naviance (a system many high schools have that is better than nothing when it comes to providing college acceptance information, but can also be very misleading in most situations).

Many students will tell me that they think they are "in the range" when they compare their GPA or test scores to the numbers they see in these systems. In the range in their opinion, means they have a good chance to be admitted. As a result, based upon the acceptance ratios of the school they are interested in, they underestimate how competitive it is and mislabel it as a match or safety rather than a reach or match. I will define this later, but I am sure you understand conceptually the terms "reach", "match" and "safety."

Unfortunately, you can't go by this, being "in the range" isn't good enough. Yes, the acceptance and decision criteria are subjective at many schools. However, being in the range isn't good enough if you want to truly understand your potential for acceptance.

There are many factors behind these numbers such as in-state versus out-of-state requirements at public schools, athletes who are recruited, majors a student chooses on their application that may be more competitive at that school, etc. For example, because the range of an ACT score for a given school is listed as being between 23 and 27 on some database that you see online, doesn't mean that because you have a 25 the school you are considering is a good match for you.

I use a proprietary system that I've had for 15 years to identify if a school is a safety, match or reach. "My" system (it is a system originally created by a very experienced mentor and now friend of mine) takes into account all students from across the country.

Then I overlay programs, Honors, early decision, early action, and majors that can impact the numbers you see online. None of the online databases that I know of account for these things which is why families are often misled. Do you need my proprietary system? Not necessarily. But you do need to understand how the school handles their incoming class, so your list is realistic, and you do not experience disappointment and frustration later on in the process.

Let's share another example. Suppose you're interested in a college and it's a smaller school, less than 5000 students. You check the numbers and see you are "in the range" online or on paper. That's great. However, let's say this specific school has a history of accepting 65% of their students, early decision. As much as you have thought about applying early decision (meaning that if you apply early decision and you are accepted you are contractually bound to attend that school regardless of where else you may be accepted) you don't plan to apply that way because you're not sure this school is a top choice and/or you may need financial aid, so you need to keep your options open.

Well, that leaves only a 35% for regular decision students, minus any special interest students the school may have, including athletes, international students, geographically diverse students, etc. These factors can obviously make the school that looks online (in general data circumstances) like they are attainable, very attainable. So, in reality, because of how the school handles their incoming class, it's actually unattainable or the chances of being accepted are much, much lower than you originally thought. The school that you categorized as a match or safety is actually now a reach.

There are other examples like state schools whom, by law, need to take a certain percentage of their students in-state versus out-of-state to receive their state and federal funding. Often times in this circumstance, the acceptance criteria for in-state students as far as GPA and test score results may also be a lot lower. However, the numbers of those in-state students are in the generic, general, universal numbers you see online.

So now you see how skewed and misleading these numbers can be if you go solely based on what is produced and published online without knowing the details.

2. Cost

If cost isn't a concern for you good for you and I wish you luck. But for those who need to be conscious of costs, finding colleges that are in your budget is no different from buying a car, a home or business.

I've always been interested in Corvettes. Since a young age I thought they were the coolest cars ever.

Now, not being a big car guy and never having spoken about horsepower, I do like cars, but cars have never been my expertise. For whatever reason, I have just loved Corvettes since I was 5-6 years old until something happened.

At a later age I found out that a 6'4" guy doesn't fit too well in a Corvette. Also, shocker here, but the cars are really expensive!

So, I realized there's really no need for me to continue to consider them from an ownership perspective. It's not the right physical or financial fit for me. I had to find other cars that I also liked and that fit me physically and financially.

I am sharing this personal interest because the concept is very relevant to the college process and when you are considering colleges to apply to. If they aren't the right financial or academic fit, why bother? You're just setting everyone up for disappointment and there is no need to do that. That is the complete opposite of making the complicated easy. It's actually making the complicated even more complicated. So please understand the way schools address financial aid and if you qualify for merit and/or other types of financial aid.

By the way, from a financial aid perspective don't assume you won't qualify for financial aid due to your income or assets. This book is not intended to get into the details of financial aid. However, you may be surprised and qualify for money that you may have thought was beyond your reach. (We have talked about this academically as well. If the types of students that apply and get accepted are high performers, maybe this means that even if you can get in, it might be a very tough road in front of you which isn't always the best idea or fit. Just because you can doesn't mean you should.

This is another lesson to keep in mind beyond your college process. Therefore, for finance, become educated so you know what to expect **before** you apply and not after. There are various ways to do this whether you calculate your expected family contribution or EFC, or you speak with the college's financial aid department to have an in-depth discussion of how they handle financial aid.

This may also include discussing financial aid options with the admissions office where different merit scholarships may be offered and where you can learn what the qualifying parameters for them may be.

3. Workload

This sounds like it's not that significant but if a student is applying to many highly selective schools, in addition to the Common Application essay, they can have 1 to 7 additional essays per school to write. Yes, I said seven. Some of these schools really make it difficult for you to apply and therefore whether the essays are 100 words, 250 words or 650 words, there's a lot of effort that goes into these essays as we will discuss shortly in detail.

And you'll be trying to get your student to do all these essays while they are trying to enjoy some well-deserved downtime during the summer, are involved in sports, including sports practices that start mid-August and/or as they start school where the more challenging class or classes they take, the summer work and actual school work they will have to do will dominate their time. Therefore, it is important to understand the essay workload for each school, so you are confident that you can get it done in the time needed without causing tremendous additional stress. But especially if there's little chance for acceptance, do you really want to do all those essays?

That's not my call because as I've said already I am not a dream crusher, and you never know what may happen. As I have said, the admission process is very subjective as we have discussed. However, how many schools fit into this category on your list? In other words, how many schools are an academic and financial reach for you?

Is it really worth it? If it's a school you've always dreamed of, by all means apply and do the essays. I tell my students that one of our top goals going through the process is that they have no regrets. But applying to a bunch of schools with little chance for acceptance is a tremendous amount of extra work and you have to really decide if it's worth it. Again, it's your call, but understand this can make a process much more complicated and stressful rather than easier, with very little upside.

There are some other factors, but these are the major mistakes many make in my opinion when putting a college list together. Apply where you want, but don't have unrealistic expectations because it will increase the stress more than what is already there. Become educated on the acceptance criteria, application workload and financial aid process so you can proactively address at least these major factors as you go through the process.

So, switching gears, how do you put a realistic college list together? I'll give you some ideas.

I tell everyone when it comes to the most selective schools in the country we can probably list them together. Though our order of which is "better" or more selective may be a little bit different, the chances of us having the same schools on the list are pretty significant. Therefore, when it comes to reaches you should follow these guidelines;

1. **No regrets.** If XYZ University or College has been your dream school for whatever reason since you were six years old, then, by all means, apply. Even if your chances are not great, you never know. Never say "what

if" when the process is done. That's my goal with all my students.

2. **Understand how the schools make admissions decisions and apply accordingly.** For example, as we discussed, if early decision is a big deal at a given school and you are in a position to apply that way, then strongly consider doing that. If not, you can still apply but know the potential impact of applying either early action or regular decision because it will probably lower your chances for acceptance.

3. **Don't apply just to be in the crowd.** There are many people applying to schools they have no business applying to. Don't do what they do just to be in the group. Apply because it's a good school for you and you have done your research. As we discussed following the herd is never a good idea.

4. **Everyone needs reaches.** So, it doesn't matter if your reach is an Ivy League school or not, reach, but reach within reason which I will also address shortly.

Now how do you find *match* schools?

We find match schools by going to visit them and doing the Vertical Visit we spoke of earlier, so we can get a good idea if you are good match for that school. But how do you determine that specifically? You determine that by establishing where you are versus the admission criteria presented by the school you're considering.

A match school is a school where you are confirming you are, "in the range". This is a school where you're at the top 75% of candidates based upon the range presented online or based upon the specific criteria you've learned from going to the school and asking specific questions. This is a school where you know not some, but many students, who had numbers similar to you who were accepted.

This is a school that you think acceptance is likely and you may even be considered for acceptance into their Honors program. These qualifications are more intense and sometimes that isn't always vividly expressed online. Therefore, you need to talk to an admissions person at the school to understand what the additional requirements are or would be for Honors consideration. Obviously overlaying the major you choose could also impact this categorization as well. If you're interested in physical therapy, those qualifications could be much different for acceptance than general admission. So, understanding that can be a big factor in confirming that a school is a match or should be put in the reach category.

Notice name was not one of the criteria I used to define a match, nor will it be for safety schools either. Match schools are colleges where your GPA and SAT or ACT scores are at the higher end of the range you gathered from that specific school. I usually identify a match school as one where I believe my student has a 65 – 80 percent chance of being admitted.

Let's define a safety school.

This is what people want to spend the least amount of time discussing. However, it's always where I want to start. I always say to my students that we want to know what their worst-case scenario is likely to be. That way, though there may be some disappointment caused by not getting into your top choice school, a great worst-case scenario that you can still be happy with will add confidence and satisfaction to the overall process.

You never want to say, "Why did I end up here with all that work I did?"

So, a safety is not the school you're better than or that you know you'll get into, but you really have no desire to go to. You can certainly find those without any help from anyone. But why apply to a college with no desire to go unless family circumstances dictate that?

College is not high school. It's hard no matter where we go as I discussed with you earlier. Don't let perceived reputation alone define your desire to attend. The fact that you are accepted and may get some money and/or were offered Honors consideration means that they actually want you. Isn't that a good thing? Plus, if you got money why not help your family out?

Don't discard the school thinking that if they offered you money you must be too smart to go there. Being wanted is always a good thing, not just in the college process, but in life. There are many advantages of being on the upper scale of your peers from an academic perspective, which by the way doesn't guarantee that you'll stay there (at the top of your school academically) but it's a great place to start.

A safety school is a school that, though it is not your top choice, you would be happy to attend if other things didn't work out as planned. If there are no schools on your list that meet that criteria, you need to continue researching and visiting schools until you have at least 2 that fit that description.

In general, for most students I suggest you apply to 2 safety schools, 6 match schools and 2 reaches. Now most people want to focus more on the reaches as we discussed, and I understand but that is very common in my 15+ years in this business. You can switch this order up in any way you wish but just understand the more reaches you have, the more important it is that your worst-case scenario is known and is an acceptable result. Understand also that the more reaches you put on your list, the more work you need to do (most likely) from an essay application perspective, and the lower likelihood that there will be merit dollars available to you and your family.

These are my general rules and guidelines for putting a realistic list of colleges together. I hope it gives you the guidance you need so you can make the process easier and achieve the results you desire.

Russ' Rules... For Staying Cool

1. Don't follow the herd.

Create a list based upon your interests not those of others who may be using criteria that will only set them up for disappointment. You can see some schools that others see but only put them on your list if they make sense for you in each category (reach, match and safety). Then also make sure that they fit your academic, social, geographic and financial parameters.

2. Make sure you use the right criteria.

Don't just go based upon the name or the fact that when you were on campus it was a sunny, fun day with students outside. You need to determine that the academic environment and social atmosphere is one that you will thrive in and that there's financial feasibility for your family. These are things you need to consider at a minimum before you apply to a school. It's not about perception of the school name that you read about or what you see on television. It's about meeting your family and student criteria and making sure that your list contains schools that are attainable at each level.

3. **Balance the list with adequate number of reaches, matches and safeties.**

> Life is about options as I always say, but you need to create them. Assuming you are realistic and have done your homework, make sure you have your worst-case scenario covered and you will be happy with that. If not, keep looking for safety and match schools that meet your criteria. Make sure you have a decent number of schools in each category for a total of between 8 to 12 schools on your final list, so at the end of the admission process you have academic, social, geographic, athletic and financial options to choose from.

COLLEGE: Making the Complicated Easy

Creating Your College List......A Deeper Dive

Because creating your college list is so critical to making the process easy (or at least easier than it can otherwise be), I wanted to share some additional information that you might find helpful. The items below are to guide you as you are creating and finalizing the college list because, again, the schools on your list will determine your ability to get admitted (your "admissibility" – don't bother looking it up, it's a word made up to capture your attention in the college arena), your ability to qualify for financial aid (the kind everyone wants; free money) and in addition to the workload (essays, supplements and applications), it will also determine your level of success and hopefully limit your degree of frustration/uncertainty.

Here are some tips on how to determine your potential to be admitted.

1-Look at the current enrolled class at the school you are considering.

Many schools provide this information online or upon request as you visit a school. Remember, being "in the range" isn't good enough if you want the school to be considered a match or safety school.

2- Understand the "competitiveness quotient".

We have discussed success and happiness quotients, but now it is time for the competitiveness quotient. The first time I heard

119 | P a g e

this phrase it was from my mentor, and now good friend. He has many years of experience in the college world at many different levels of involvement. He is a great guy and has so much experience and knowledge, it is amazing!

Anyway, you must determine the competiveness of certain majors you are considering, schools within the university you are applying to (i.e., the business school versus the arts and science school) and athletic ability (if it applies), etc. The higher you are on these factors compared to those who were accepted before you, the greater your chances for admission and therefore the higher your competiveness quotient. The lower you are as compared to the same group, the lower your competitiveness quotient. Obviously, you want a high competitiveness quotient if you want a higher likelihood of acceptance.

3-You have to ask for other unknown factors.

You ask the admissions contacts, the financial aid counselors, the heads of a department, the coach and so on. Don't assume all information you need is published because it isn't. Having conversations with people in positions of knowledge at the college is important to make sure your ratings and categorizations are accurate.

List Creation Thoughts

Never apply to a college that you wouldn't enroll in if accepted.

This may sound obvious but a pet peeve of mine is when students apply to a school that they are very confident they will get admitted to, but they do it only as a safety (they have no intention of attending). As we discussed, there are many schools out there. You can find reach, match and safety schools for you no matter what your academic achievements are. Applying to a school just to say you were accepted, with no intention of actually going, really is a waste of time for you and it impacts others' chances for admission when they really want to attend. I always say, "Not my money, not my child" when it comes to advising my families and making suggestions. I say this to emphasize that my intentions are not to overstep or to tell them what to do. But this is something I strongly advise against doing.

Don't look for the "right" college, meaning the one school that "is it".

I understand that we all want to be excited about the schools we are applying to, and you should be. However, though you may have a favorite, or two, I believe that there is no ONE school that is the "right" school. If you go through the process as we have discussed, you should have several or many schools that meet your criteria.

Create your student's criteria for a school that interests them and a number system to rate one against another.

Create Your Student's Criteria (Family Criteria too)

- The academic rigor - is it a match or is it more difficult than others?

- Do they offer the major(s) you are interested in?

- Is the size and geography reasonable?

- Are the average class sizes and ability to get help when needed acceptable?

- Are the living accommodations acceptable, convenient?

- Is the social and cultural environment a good match for you? (Greek system, technological school, etc.)

- Is there a campus or not, is that important to you?

- Are there extracurricular activities that interest you and what is the process to be included?

- Are there special learning and academic support resources available and how available are they?

- Cost and financial aid, does the likely cost match your budget?

- Athletics – can you play, or will you be given an opportunity to earn your spot or will you likely be on the bench?

- Reputation – We discussed this at length. Be careful with this one. It's not all about a name. Make sure the name follows through in every way to be worthy of that name (and the likely cost).

Furthermore, there are **4 Critical Questions** to ask to ensure you are considering the schools that make sense for you and your family. Though I suppose there may be others you could add, these are the questions that I use with my clients to ensure we are on track.

Question #1 - Is the school the right Academic Fit?

As we have discussed in several contexts, making sure a school is the right academic fit is important. It is really not only about getting in. I know that sounds counterintuitive but it's true.

COLLEGE: Making the Complicated Easy

Most people say they want to get into and go to, "the best school they can get into". Then most define that as the school with the best brand name which often also comes with an increased difficulty to get admitted and price tag.

I'm just going to say again, college is not high school. It's hard! The level of difficulty and rigor is something you need to gauge to ensure the student can handle the workload. I can't tell you how many students come back to me to tell me how hard their college experience is. Parents also tell me how much their kids are struggling with college level work. Remember, the goal is not to get in. It's to get in, learn, challenge yourself without overwhelming yourself, graduate in 4 years, find a major that interests you, have a positive social experience and get a job upon graduation. I wish everyone looked at it this way, but many don't.

You also should understand if a specific school is a reach, match or safety, so you don't get carried away seeing schools that make your list lopsided with reaches. This could mean you are looking at colleges that aren't a great academic fit for you.

Is the school a good Environmental Fit?

It is important that the student is in a social atmosphere that is synergistic with their personality. The student should feel that they will fit in comfortably in a reasonable amount of time. Transitions aren't easy for most people. However, they go easier when you're in the right environment socially, geographically, culturally and otherwise.

Academics are important but we all know the happier you are in your non-academic world, the better you will do in that academic world.

123 | P a g e

Is the school the right Financial Fit?

The college a student attends should be within the family budget. Just because a school costs more doesn't mean it's better. You need to understand how the financial elements work. You should have a good idea of what you can expect from a financial aid perspective before a student applies and certainly before you make a final college decision. Calculate your EFC (Expected Family Contribution), understand how aid is addressed by the school and if merit dollars are possible.

Is the school the right Admissions Fit?

Does the student have a good chance of being admitted? What are your sources to confirm this? Does the opportunity get impacted by admissions strategy (early decision, early action) and how does that impact your potential to get admitted (and financial aid)?

Also, make sure there are several schools that meet the admission criteria strongly, so you have a good idea that the student will be accepted, so you have options that are good for the student and family. Safety, Match and Reach, address each in this order rather than the inverse.

The Most Avoided Strategy - Not having a strong Plan B

Look, I know everyone wants to plan for the best outcome and I hope that happens for you. That does happen for many of my students. However, regardless, as I said, I make sure we have a strong worst-case scenario.

As we discussed earlier, most people don't want to think about that but it's important to have the worst-case scenario cared for, so you have confidence that things are going to go well.

Finding this next tier of schools and a couple that you feel very happy about sometimes can be more challenging than finding reaches. Aside from the lack of glamour associated with doing this, it also becomes an attitudinal thing thinking the school isn't good enough for you. I'm here to tell you, it most likely is. Spend time finding them as well and don't just fill this end of your list with schools you have no intention to attend.

<u>Russ Rules... For Staying Cool</u>

1. Ask yourself the 4 important college questions

2. Constantly assess your admissibility and competitiveness quotient

3. Understand the impact of different admissions options and major choices

4. Start with a rather large list, hone it down using your criteria, expand the list a little and then finalize it

5. Match schools against your criteria as a way to hone, expand and finalize your list (as well as when making an attending decision)

6. Decide how many applications essays you want to complete, and make sure you plan properly so you have time to put your best foot forward for admission

Four Seconds! Really?

"The essay is the one place you can show them who you really are"

- Russ

I read that there was a survey done several years ago, finding that college admission's people take 4 seconds, yes FOUR seconds, to decide if they're going **to read or scan** the main essay of the student's college application. Now I've told all my clients that I believe that a student is either on the potential acceptance pile or not based upon their standardized test scores and GPA. Nothing against Key Club, but that is not the reason a student is considered for acceptance. Don't get me wrong, belonging to a club or doing community service is important and altruistic so I do believe that doing these things are important.

However, it's the GPA, standardized test scores and rigor of classes taken, that carry the most weight when it comes to the final admissions decision, no matter what a college tells you when you visit them. I say this because many colleges say that they "look at the whole student" when making a college admission decision.

But colleges are receiving so many applications year after year and typically aren't staffed properly to review every application holistically. So, despite them saying at an information session that they look at the whole student, I find that very hard to believe. Especially at very competitive schools, they want you to apply because of the way bogus rating systems work. They need you to apply, and if they told you how tough it was to get in, you might decide it's not worth it and by not applying you hurt their rankings. By the way, I don't necessarily fault the colleges because I understand that they have to play the game, or their enrollments can suffer. However, I think this misleads people to have more unrealistic goals. When families hear from someone in admissions that they look at more than test scores families automatically think it means they really do have a chance.

This is a whole different topic we can discuss another time but my net advice to you is; don't believe that they look at the whole student. I am sure some may, but I am pretty confident a majority don't.

Further proof of this opinion is supported by two things. First, most colleges are asking for less letters of recommendation. It used to be three in total; one from a guidance counselor and two from teachers. Now, if they are requested at all, as some schools have actually dropped this requirement entirely, it's one or maybe two letters of recommendation rather than three. I believe this is for a couple reasons.

Again, they don't have the staff or the time to read all these letters, and they know that these letters typically add little value in understanding more about the student. I mean, what can you say about each student if you are a teacher that is so unique and different?

How can you say to an admissions person, "Oh yeah, this is your guy or girl?" Therefore, letters of recommendation are an administrative component but not typically a deal breaker or maker in the process, in my opinion. Second, a recent survey was done stating that colleges (on average) spend eight minutes, yes 8 minutes not hours, reviewing a student's application for admission. Can you believe that? You spend all this time working on your application(s) and they give you 8 minutes? For many of the same reasons I stated above with the letters of recommendation, how holistic of a review can you do in eight minutes?

Anyway, with that said I tell all my students that if they make it past the first two criteria (which again is GPA and standardized test scores, with the exception of SAT optional schools) the next two criterion they emphasize is the rigor of the classes you have taken that are on your transcript and **the most important aspect of the application process; the essays**.

As we discussed in the last chapter relative to creating your college list, assuming you took my advice and created a realistic list, the other thing the list drives is the essay workload. We will get into detail now on how to approach this critical part of the application and admission process.

Since it is so important I host an essay and application workshop (actually three or four of them) each year depending on how many students I have in a given year. These workshops are for the student and parent (or parents) to attend.

During these workshops, I explain how we are going to work together over the summer and into the fall of application season. In addition, I share the many other tips and steps I will use to help them manage and alleviate their stress during this busy and work intensive time.

Despite essays being very time consuming and challenging in multiple ways, these are one of my client's favorite activities. We create a plan for what and when things need to be done, from June until it is time to apply.

But what I spend the most time on is covering the do's and don'ts, sample essay reviews and sharing the current year's essay topics so kids and parents understand what the essays are supposed to be about.

I emphasize the significance of their essays and I also tell them that their essays are their only opportunity to share details on who they are, how they feel, what they think, what they bring or can contribute to the college community, and so on.

It's an excellent opportunity to represent themselves in a way that is unique to them and to tell the college admission board what is special about them outside of their list of activities and academic achievements.

Therefore, I spend a lot of time on these essays. It's the most labor-intensive and mentally challenging thing I do, because I work so closely with my students and dig deep, which in some cases is incredibly challenging. Teenagers aren't always anxious to get personal and share details, especially if they have to talk about it rather than post it somewhere. However, I love it because it's an opportunity to be creative and for me to get to know my students very well personally.

It's where our bond gets closer and deeper because we share, talk and brainstorm about personal events, feelings and experiences that have helped create the person that they are today. I tell each of my students that their essays will not be scanned!! They deserve better and full attention for all the work they put in, not four seconds.

So therefore, we work towards creating the best damn essay we can. One that is entertaining to read, revealing regarding their personal attributes and, dare I say, we are going to have fun doing it.

Often, they don't believe me when I say this out loud, but I would say at least 8 out of 10 students I work with end up saying I was right. After we find a topic for them most enjoy writing it much more than they thought.

Also, it is important to note that they obviously write the essays in their voice and style which is a challenge when parents read them. The help I provide is generating ideas and helping them express themselves. **It is not writing it for them or modifying things, so it is no longer their essay(s).** This is a requirement for all the students I work with despite some parents wanting to doctor the essays up using big words and writing things in a 40-50-year-old perspective. Also, believe it or not, because the essays are personal, sometimes the student may have difficulty sharing it with their parents. I work with my students to come up with the right topic and to help them get their words on paper, but I also require that they share their essay with their parents before it is final for many reasons.

Several are listed below;

A parent may learn about their child's thoughts, feelings and activities as well as experiences that they didn't initially know about because there's little communication between them at home. Anyone with a teenager can relate to this on some level. You wouldn't think it would be true, however I found it to be true many more times than I originally thought.

Parents know the child best in most cases despite what a student may think. So, often times a parent can add value with ideas and tidbits the student didn't think of when they read the essay and are aware of the topic. Often, they may try too hard to interject their opinions which can create other challenges I need to deal with on occasion.

But typically, I'm pretty good at it. Making sure that neither the parents nor I overstep as far as our help and influence on these essays, is something I pay very close attention to.

Parents pay for my services, so I believe they absolutely deserve to see the final product, essays and applications. I guess despite being the Cool College Guy most times, in this respect I'm somewhat old-school.

Even though it's not the case, I will not be put in a position where parent says their student did not get accepted into their first-choice college because of their essay topic or topics. This is something I may receive as feedback if the parent does not have the opportunity to read it, provide input and approve the essay. As I said before, I don't believe this to be true because I would never suggest a student write about something inappropriate. However, parents react in many odd ways if their child doesn't get into their top choice school. Therefore, I make sure that parents read the essay and give their approval, so we are all on the same page. That way we all agree that they are putting their best foot forward regarding the student's positioning for admission.

A side note for parents; it can be hard letting go and having your child write the essay. You might be tempted to micromanage them at times. I understand this, but it is critical that you don't get too involved and don't make the essay more yours than theirs. Their essay, as I've said, is one of the most difficult things for a student to do. Any feedback, and I mean any feedback, that you give can and most likely will be taken as criticism no matter how gently you try to deliver it. That's why I advise my parents to provide me with their feedback rather than providing it directly to their child. This way I can either explain to them why we shouldn't or can't include their (parent) ideas or possibly use their suggestions and share them with my student.

If a parent does make good content suggestions I usually can introduce them in a much more casual way with my students. Typically, by asking the student questions and having the student provide me feedback is where I can get them to *buy in* to the concept. That way they actually embrace the concept or idea that the parent had in a way that makes them feel it was something they came up with themselves. We all know as parents that many times news and advice delivered by outside resources, even if they say it exactly as we have, is received more favorably by our children.

If you don't get outside help or feedback on the essay, that is fine, because it isn't always necessary to do so. However, absolutely parents, under no circumstance, do you write or rewrite your child's essay. Though it is expected that there's more thought, time, and effort that go into these essays as compared to, for example their standardized test essays, they (admissions) can tell if a student wrote their essay or if it has been doctored tremendously by some outside resource.

Keeping the essay in the student's style and voice is critical. Believe me using big words or phrases that are adult-ish in terminology and context will stand out in a negative way. Anytime I can tell an essay has received outside help I call my students out on it.

Many schools may expect that students get help from English teachers (which also would enable them to do some polishing) but it is important in this case too that the student's voice remains constant throughout the essay.

There have been times I have had to call the parents of a student, so they understand why their attempt to help is very counterproductive in their child's college admission process and in their consideration for admission.

Some of these conversations have been very entertaining and interesting over the years.

But I typically get my point across and represent my students in the most reasonable and protective manner. Therefore, parents please let your child be the best version of them without significant help from you or people who claim to be college essay specialists.

It's great training for students being themselves, learning independence, and going through the first of many steps they'll be facing when they start their college years and beyond.

My process personified – when I work with students, they write their essays and that should go without saying based upon what I just covered. But I wanted to state that again very clearly for those who think people like me are involved and influence the final product more than I do. Yes, I help students brainstorm and come up with topics they embrace. Yes, I push them in a way others can't, to make the essays personal, fun and significant. However, I follow the same general guidance that I suggest to all parents. The essays need to stay authentic and in the student's voice and style.

So how do I do this without overstepping? I tell my students to pick a topic and just write. I don't care if they think it's terrible. It doesn't matter if it's too long, (meaning over the word limit in the first draft). It doesn't matter if it sounds negative. I ask them to just write it with no pressure or criticism.

That way they say and share all the details the way they want to, so it all comes out and I can learn as much as I can about them as well as why they chose the topic that they did.

Then we discuss it, why they chose the topic, and what they want it to say about them. We also collectively make suggestions on what the next steps are after a long conversation and mutual sharing. This works well in most cases and takes all the pressure off them, so they don't overthink or judge themselves on their first attempts at their essays.

My favorite story regarding the essay process is one I share every year with my students at the essay and application workshop. I share this to show them that I'm not kidding about having them just writing whatever and as much as they want for their first draft. This helps assure them that we will be able to find a topic that works for them no matter what they write about.

So, years ago I had a client who I built a close relationship with. We talked about many things, she asked and shared many things with me, and we were both pretty sarcastic, so there was no shortage of humorous banter back-and-forth, which we both enjoyed. Anyway, she came to meet with me about her essay with her first draft in hand.

She walked into my office with confidence and attitude. I started laughing and she threw a three-page essay on the desk, sat down in the chair on the other side of my desk, and said, "Here, read it!" I grabbed it and started reading and she sat there with her arms crossed, staring at me looking for a glimpse of anything that might give her an idea regarding my opinion of her "masterpiece". After I read it she said, "So what do you think?" I asked her if she wanted me to be honest with her and she said, "Of course, honestly. Do you know another way?"

And she was right so we both laughed, and I then told her that it sucked. Now I wouldn't say this to all my students but as I said she and I had a close relationship plus I knew her well enough to know she was not going to run out of my office crying. She couldn't believe that I meant it, so she continued to ask me, "Wait, it sucks?"

She then went on to tell me that she used big words that she thought sounded impressive. I responded saying that there are big words but since she doesn't really talk that way it probably meant she was trying too hard. Also, I told her that her attempt to impress XYZ college with big words, and trying to sound extra smart, was likely to fail in impressing them but also fail in keeping her authenticity.

She was very dejected at this point and she said "Well, can you tell me something? Did you like any of it? Honestly?" So, I told her that I liked two sentences. Hey, I was being honest. Her mouth gaped open and she was in utter disbelief that I only liked two sentences out of three pages.

She said. "Are you kidding me?" and she burst out laughing. The reality was that the essay was well written, and I liked other parts. However, two sentences really jumped out at me and I wanted to discuss them with her. I explained to her that, "You are one of the most vibrant kids I know."

It was true. When she walked into a room her presence was known in a natural and good way. I told her that I wanted people to know and feel that about her when they read her essay. She had so much to offer but in her *canned* essay I felt she was being artificial, and she was anything but that in person. I told her what I tell all of my students. I told her that I wanted everyone who read her essay to know how amazing she is because that's what I think.

That's what I wanted to come across loud and clear in her essay as I try to do with every one of my students.

She got a big smile across her face which was vastly different from her original scowl. She unconsciously had been listening but all of a sudden it was like a light bulb went off. After she observed and moved on from my first couple of harsh words I could see that she was ready to go. She saw what I meant and wanted to know what part I liked. I told her which two sentences, yes two sentences out of three pages, I liked.

She smiled, asked why and we spent the next 10 to 15 minutes talking about it and how she could expand upon it. Her whole essay became about these two sentences. It is still one of my favorite essays today and I share it every year with every one of my students. It's unique, it's fun, funny at certain times, entertaining and you learn great things about her in almost every sentence.

Several of the colleges she applied to, and was accepted to, wrote notes to her saying how much they enjoyed her essay. Now I understand that writing essays is a subjective process. I talk to my kids and my parents about that all the time. I'm sure we've all Googled the best college essays and read them. I know I have. But many times, after I read them I find myself saying, "Are you kidding? Really?" But in this instance, it was obvious that her essay was read and that they (the colleges she applied to) truly enjoyed reading it. The comments she received were truly thoughtful, complimentary and encouraging.

And that is my goal with every student I work with! That is what I would like your goal to be when you write your essay(s). Don't settle on a topic or just look to get it done. Dig deeper and find something that is fun and unique about you. You don't need a life impacting event.

Don't think your life is too boring because nothing terrible happened to you yet.

I mean, that's actually a great thing. If you have had a "normal", "boring" life thus far as many of my students initially say to me, good for you. However, that doesn't mean you have nothing to share or offer the world. This brainstorming I do with my students is fun, challenging at times but also energizing for me and them. I can't tell you how many times a discouraged student enters my office and after we do this together, they tell me they can't wait to get started writing about their new topic.

So therefore, when I work with my students, do I help them? Yes, I do. But I help them to find a topic that they feel good about, passionate about, excited to write about, and then I let them go. I help them see how amazing they are and how they should let the world know it.

I would like to briefly mention the timing of the essay process, so you know when to start and fit it into your college planning calendar. I typically start the essay writing process with my students in June of their junior year.

I do this because school is winding down, so they should have more time to fit it in to the busy lives. I also do it because I want them still in school mode when we start writing. Similar to the simulated tests we discussed, mindset is important. So proper timing is critical to get the best effort from my students.

I also start in June because it takes time; sometimes a lot of time. There usually are several drafts done, edits made and sometimes major shifts that the student makes as they go through the essay writing process. Also, in addition to what I will call the main essay (Common Application essay) many schools have supplemental essays they require as well. Therefore, depending on the schools a student is applying to, their workload (again driven by their list) can vary and may increase greatly.

This makes starting early even more important, so they are making the potentially complicated easier by working on the essays over time rather than crunching it all into the month they are hitting the submit button.

Another very important point I would like to make is that a college application essay is not an English paper. Every year I have students tell me that they did their college essay in English class. You would think more English classes would include this as part of their curriculum, but most don't, so the number of students stating this to me is not large at all. It is actually the exception rather than the rule in most cases. Despite many of the papers that were written in English class receiving very respectable grades, I always tell my students I would like to read it before we decide it is done.

I have to say that there was not one time that one of these papers were used as they were submitted in English class. This is nothing against English teachers at all. I am just saying that often times I feel there can be more creativity, less need for the traditional structure and more personalization that can be added to most essays I see.

Now, writing is subjective. If you showed an essay to 10 different people, you will probably get 10 different ratings and responses. But that being said, I have found that the essays often lack depth and self-reflection. They often just scratch the surface of where they should and could be in my opinion. I will tell you that this essay is supposed to be engaging enough to keep the admissions person's attention.

It is supposed to help them make a solid decision regarding your ability to fit in, contribute and make it there.

Therefore, it needs to be strong, personal and show details about who you are. I tell all my students they need to show, not tell, in their essay. Everyone, even if it is not true, will say they are responsible, disciplined and they work hard. When writing a college essay, you need to do more than just make claims. You need to show that the claims you make are legit and true to whom you really are.

Just to show you the kind of things I get handed in to me at times, I will give you one extreme example that I had a couple years back. I had a new student come to me a bit late in the process looking for help. I asked her about the essay and where she was with it. She told me it was done, and she got a 94 on it from her English teacher. In my normal process, I told her that was great, but I would like to read it.

The topic was that she gets car sick. Now this may have had some potential if it were meant to be a humorous piece. However, this was very serious, and she used the word "vomit" 5 times in the first paragraph alone.

As I was reading I started to get visuals in my head and actually started feeling a little queasy. If you have ever been in the vicinity of someone who was sick in this way you know what I am talking about. Just being near them or hearing them can start to give you uneasy feelings. This is bad enough if it is someone you love that is sick. But if you are an admissions person, do you want those visuals in your head about a student you are considering for acceptance?

If you are a student, do you want admissions to think of you in a queasy manner every time they see your name? Needless to say, despite the 94, we changed her essay completely so admissions would actually enjoy her essay and have nothing but positive thoughts when they thought of her.

College essays are one of the most challenging and labor-intensive parts of the process for students and whomever they have helping them (parent or outside facilitator). It's true for me too, but it's the one time of year I look forward to every year when it comes to my business. It enables me to connect with my students in a way I hadn't yet. And it enables me to learn more about them, where they came from, and what's important to them. I also get to see them develop and grow as they progress through the process.

Whether they were fully engaged in their journey, enjoying their polishing of the essay that they are now doing, or if they were somewhat resistant to their upcoming college voyage. It really doesn't matter because I know as we go through the essay process, they now feel much better about it, and in more control. This comes from them actively participating in the creation, editing, and finalizing their essays.

It's one of the most enlightening and enjoyable parts of the process for me despite the incredible amounts of effort and time that goes into each one. There are books written about writing college essays, so I am choosing to stop here because we have other things to address. However, it is my hope that I have provided you with enough guidance and perspective that you can go forward and conquer the college essay with confidence.

Russ' Rules… For Staying Cool

1. Make the Common Application Essay personal and engaging.

This essay is the best opportunity to share who you are, what is important to you and what you are about. Don't waste it talking too much about other people or chronologically listing things that happened. Give admissions an opportunity to learn about you. I have said this many times to my students, and I have heard admissions people say the same in Information Sessions, "If I found your essay on the floor with no name on it, after I am done reading it, would I be able to know who the essay belongs to?" It is not an English essay, so you don't have to be formal. Write it, be specific and try to have fun with it.

2. It is okay to get help writing the essay.

Whether it is an English teacher you trust, your parent or someone else, it is okay to get feedback and confirmation that you are on the right track. They can help you with brainstorming ideas or with other aspects as needed. However, make sure the essay is in your (the student's) voice. Make sure it says what you want it to say. You don't want to lose your authenticity and genuine tone by having others over-edit what you have written. Make sure YOU are happy with the final result. Everyone has a story to tell. Share how awesome you are without being overconfident. Share details without listing each and every step. Have fun with it, use humor if you can, be creative and make sure the admissions person feels great about you after they read it.

3. Writing the essays takes time. Make sure you make the time to do them right.

In addition to the Common Application essay there may be supplements, personal statements and other writing required depending upon the schools you are applying to. Writing these essays takes time, especially if writing isn't your favorite thing to do. I start the essay writing process with my clients in June of their junior year and we work on them throughout the summer and early fall of their senior year. As much as you can get done before fall athletic practices and school starts the better.

Believe me, you will be glad you started early, and in the theme of making the process "easy" you will have done that by allowing adequate time to get things done and not leaving it all until the last minute.

Let Me Introduce Myself

"Interviews won't make or break you,
but they should be done."

Russ

The interview. Many people no matter what their age, fear the interview. What do I say? What if they ask me something I don't know? Will they like me? Was I boring? Did I talk too much? All these questions go through people's minds before and after any interview.

With the college interview, there's an added complexity because teenagers are usually more comfortable texting their words rather than saying them. I'm sure as a parent you know that all too well. As one who works with teens every day, I see this more and more. So, to set the record straight regarding the college interview, let's clear up a couple of things.

First, do you have to do it? I always suggest to my clients that they do an interview if it is made available to them. Nowadays, interviews aren't typically evaluative (meaning they aren't a key criterion for admission), rather they are informative. This means that they are for both parties (the college and the student) to learn more about each other and to identify if the school is a good academic, social, and geographic fit.

Therefore, if a school offers an interview, and especially if the school is a top choice, the student should interview at the college. This can get a little crazy if many of the colleges you are considering do conduct interviews. I suggest that my students interview at all schools that offer it. But if they are limited on time or resources, they should interview at a minimum, at their top 4 choices. This includes reaches, but it should also include match and safety schools as well. This way you don't make a college where you feel pretty confident about being admitted feel like they aren't significant to you, which could negatively impact your chances for admission.

In general, the reason you want to interview is to show your interest in the school and to learn more about it. Even if it is not a major criterion to the admission process, you should show your interest and learn more before you apply or before you attend.

This can only help you in making a final college decision if you are admitted. In addition, if a college is trying to decide which of two candidates they are going to admit, and everything is pretty much the same, but one interviewed and one didn't, who would you accept? Also, assuming colleges have effective communications between interviewers and admission, taking the one candidate who went that extra mile to show their interest and learn more about the school is a no brainer. Just sayin'…

One major reason that students have for not being interested in an interview is the nervousness they feel about the whole interview process. To address the anxiety and outright panic I see some students have with an interview, I would like to introduce the second bit of advice regarding a college interview.

I want you to know there's only one way to screw up a college interview. The only way you can mess up in a college interview would be if you actually said these words, "This school sucks and I'm not going here!"

This is literally what I tell all my clients as I prepare them for an interview. Of course, they laugh as I hope you did, but that's the point. I see their shoulders slide back down where they should be and the air return to their lungs as I say this to them. I mean this quite literally even though I also say this to my students to break the ice and put them at ease. Typically, the interviewer is not trying to stump you or trick you. They may want to see how you think on your feet.

Maybe they want to see how creative you are. But trying to catch you shouldn't be in their plan when conducting an interview. I have been told many times by my students that they thought about what I said to them and they literally laughed going into the interview. As a result, they were so much more relaxed.

They have also shared that most times, the interview went better than they expected. This is because they were better prepared and more competent than they thought, but also because most interviewers interview because they enjoy it. So, they make it a relaxed, informal atmosphere. That way talking, and sharing is not high pressure. Now, that being said, there are ways to excel in the interview which we will discuss shortly. But bombing it is really hard to do. Please know that and go a little easier on yourself in your preparation and mindset before doing a college interview.

Third, I don't know of any interviews in the college process that are truly evaluative, meaning they are a leading admissions criteria and a reason a student was not accepted to the school of their choice.

I know I briefly mention this above, but it is important enough to restate.

It is not likely that doing well means you are in or doing poorly means you are out. Most interviews are again informative, meaning they aim to provide the admissions candidate with solid information about the school as well as allow the candidate to ask questions.

From the questions they ask you want to gather as much information as you can to either validate if it is a good choice for you or have you think twice about applying. With today's emphasis on silly ratings, which I don't support in any meaningful way, colleges mostly want a student to apply even if their chances for admission are slim. I won't get into this here but take my word for it. It's another reason many schools offer you an opportunity to apply when you visit, or they offer to waive the application fee. Therefore, if it's not a key determinant, a student should absolutely prepare and try their best, but like everything I've discussed in this book, there's no reason to stress or lose sleep as long as you follow my tips to make it easy.

Last, it is important to know if a college you are considering offers an interview. Obviously, you can go on the college website for that specific school to see what you can find out. However, I also suggest that my students reach out to their admissions contact so they can ask if, when and what the process is for an interview. Some schools interview whenever you are able to be on campus. Some colleges interview only during summer months.

Some colleges interview only after you apply. Some colleges only choose random students to interview. Some colleges have alumni conduct the interviews locally. Some may offer Skype interviews. Don't assume.

Talk with admissions, and make sure for each college you know if, when and what the process is for an interview.

Here are some important tips on how to properly prepare but not have an anxiety attack when you are on your college interview.

1. Research the school so you know why you'd want to go there.

> This sounds obvious, but it goes further than that. The reason you want to go to specific college is not because "it just felt right". As we talked about in the visitation section it is true that students sometimes feel that way. There are students who when they walk on a given campus say that they just knew it was the right fit for them. That's okay when the student is doing their own internal or family assessment of the school.
>
> However, in an interview this is clearly not going to give the interviewer any details on not only why you're interested but how involved you were in the visitation and information gathering process.
>
> Therefore, do research on the school website, do online searches and use other sources to get a feel for the school academically, socially, athletically, geographically and financially, which is critically important.
>
> From this research, you should have some idea of the things you found interesting in all of those categories and use the interview to validate those findings and

assumptions. Make sure the school has the things you want (and you assume are available) while you're in the interview so if you attend the college, there are no big surprises.

2. While doing research is a must, and gathering information is important, don't expect or try to know everything.

It is impossible to be an expert on a given school. Even if your family went there, you have visited 4 times and have done extensive research, come prepared but use the interview to learn more and gather new information as well. The point of the interview is for you to gain information and then validate the information with your interviewer to make sure you're using the right assumptions and criteria for ranking a school in regards to its attractiveness to you. So, do research, prepare well, but also don't put pressure on yourself expecting that you will know everything.

3. Dress appropriately.

It doesn't matter who the interviewer is, whether it is an admissions counselor, a student, or an alumnus, you only have one chance to make a good impression. This is true in the college interview as it is in life. Therefore, don't wear jeans, shorts, tank tops, flip flops, sneakers, or inappropriate clothing of any sort. In general, wear what you would if you were going to church or synagogue. Not overdone with a suit and tie, or fancy dress, but neat, and not too casual.

Every year I have students, especially my boys, who will say "I saw kids that were in shorts, tank tops, and hats on backwards". And I'll say, "Well that's good for them because that means you should've made a great impression. You stood out from everybody else. So, you can thank them and me for not being like them." Dressing appropriately shows you are taking your interview time seriously and also puts you in the right mindset for the event. More on mindset later on.

4. Don't be late.

This sounds obvious too, but it doesn't matter if we're talking about your interview, a meeting with others, or an appointment, such as with the doctor, dentist, lawyer or for that matter, me! Arriving 10 minutes late is not okay. For that matter, arriving at 10 AM when your appointment is at 10 AM is also not acceptable in my opinion. You should arrive 15 minutes early even if the people you're meeting with run late. To set the tone so your interviewer knows your serious, and so you have time to relax, get your thoughts together, and possibly gain an advantage, you should arrive early.

This also may be greatly appreciated by your interviewer if they are running ahead of time or even if they are running late. By arriving early and being flexible, you have a great opportunity to get on the right, or good side, of the interviewer and start the interview on a very positive note which is incredibly important.

5. Don't lie.

What? I know you would never lie. I'm sure most you would never lie. And I'm sure most of you would not lie and you shouldn't. But even the most honest student may be tempted if facing a question, they don't know how to answer. I mean, let's face it, this is an interview for an academic purpose and you want to look smart enough to go there right? So, saying "I don't know" may make you look unqualified, right? Wrong.

You're not going to say it that way at all. If you don't know the answer to something (not because you don't feel like being creative or you think their question is ridiculous) because it's about a subject you aren't well educated on, don't make things up. It'll catch you 8 times out of 10. When they ask a follow-up question on that same subject that you can't answer, or you answer incorrectly, it is going to be obvious you weren't truthful.

What you should say instead when asked a question you are not sure how, or if you can, answer, is something like this, "I apologize but I'm not familiar with that. Can you explain it to me a little bit further please?" Or say this, "I'm sorry I probably should know more about that, but I don't at the moment. Can you share some information with me, so I can try to answer that question?" Both responses work well. If they tell you not to worry about it, write it down, do research when you go home, and write it in you thank you email with a brief synopsis and another short apology for not being able to answer it in person. Provide your new opinion or feedback based upon the research that you've done.

This shows your commitment to being perceived positively, your thoroughness in making sure they know it was important to you, and maturity by taking accountability and using your intellectual curiosity to fix the problem. No one knows everything.

Therefore, it's okay to say you are not prepared to answer a question. It's how you proceed from there that really matters.

6. Have a list of questions with you. That way when you are asked if you have any questions at the end of your interview, your answer isn't, "Umm, no."

I usually suggest having at least three questions in each of the following categories; admissions process, academics, and social environment. It's important to them that you show your preparedness and that you are serious.

These questions can be about anything. Here are some examples;

- Do many students go home on weekends?
- Can you tell me about how students participate in clubs, athletic and otherwise? Is it open acceptance or is there a process for participating?
- I was thinking about majoring in Biology. Can you tell me about the medical school application process?
- I would be interested in an internship, so I can get experience in my major. Can you tell me what the process is for getting an internship?
- I know that this school seems to accept a lot of students applying early decision. Am I at a great disadvantage if I don't apply early decision?

These are just some examples. However, you can literally ask anything you want if it helps you confirm your assumptions, or it will help you get a better idea regarding the school's compatibility with you.

BONUS QUESTION FOR YOU TO ASK: This is the one question I suggest every student ask while they are in an interview. Ready?

The one most important question that in my opinion is mandatory is; *"Knowing what you've learned about me here today, is there anything you would suggest I do to improve my chances for admission?"* Yes, you can ask this. Now don't expect to get a "golden nugget" here necessarily. You are likely to get a generic answer or be pushed strongly to consider early decision if they offer it. You probably knew that before you went in for the interview. But that's the worst-case scenario. It is possible that you will or may get some advice relative to what you have discussed during the interview that could help with the application and admission process. It's important to write the advice down (if you do receive it) and discuss it with your parents or advisor when you get home. That way you can include it somewhere in your application.

7. Bring a resume.

> To be clear, I'm not big on submitting resumes in the application process. The only times I suggest my students submit a resume is if they have many significant activities that don't fit on their application, or if the activities they list include very significant involvement that requires more space to be explained. This is when your responsibilities and experiences are so great that the limitations often included in the application as far as characters or word counts will not allow you to include everything the way you would like to explain it.

> However, when you interview, I feel it is important to have something to give your interviewer. Most students

will not have one, so it's a way to stand out as well. But also, it'll be something the interviewer can access, take notes on and add to your file. They can also use it to form questions that are aimed specifically at subjects that you're very familiar with (or should be) so you can talk about them in greater detail. The resume doesn't have to be fancy, but it should be clean, neatly organized, and clear. It's a nice touch.

8. Send a follow-up thank you note via email.

To do so make sure you get the interviewers contact information including their email address before you leave the interview. Many of my students don't do that despite me telling them to do so because they think they can find it online. DON'T DO THIS PLEASE. Ask before you leave so you have it and so you can write a thank you note, address any open items that you would like to clarify or items you would like to emphasize again. This will also enable you to keep the communication lines open as you go through the application process which can only help.

9. Last and very important, have confidence that you belong there and will have a good interview!

Your interviewer can be bubbly and fun or can be all business and dry. I can tell you regardless of how they behave or conduct themselves it most likely has nothing to do with you. Prepare as we have discussed, practice in front of a mirror your responses (please see the insert below), practice with friends or family and go in there (not cocky) confident.

Be you.

I know you want this. If you didn't, you wouldn't be there in the first place, but don't change who you are just to try to fit in. Be your awesome self and if they like you fantastic! Why wouldn't they? But if you get the feeling they don't, or they are unimpressed by you (because this can happen) you alone can decide if you want or need to do more research on the school to determine if it's still a good match for you, or if it's time to move on.

Talk with people that you know in this case, maybe visit the school again, and talk to students who attend. See if your opinions on the school have changed because of the conversation, because now you are looking at different criteria. Be you, be confident, enjoy the interview, follow up after, take notes, and proceed accordingly.

Good luck!!

I mentioned practicing your responses in front of a mirror, out loud by the way! This may sound silly, but I give my clients a list of common questions and tell them to do this as well. Listen, I am ridiculously comfortable speaking in front of people. I tell people, not to brag, but to make my point. I literally could (and have) been asked last minute to fill in for an hour in front of an audience with no prior preparation or knowledge that I would need to make a presentation. I can do it happily and well. But despite my comfort level with this scenario, I practice (out loud) usually when I'm in my car. This includes presentations and sometimes even customer meetings. I have even practiced important conversations with my daughter this way but don't tell her that.

I have always done this, and prior to Bluetooth and modern technology, you could probably imagine the looks I got as people would see me talking to myself, animated, and with a huge smile on my face most of the time. Nowadays though, people don't even notice as I do the same. However, I do this not to entertain other cars on the road but to hear myself, my message, my examples, and even my jokes out loud.

A lot of the time things sound different when you hear them read out loud. So, I test the theory to make sure everything sounds right. You should do the same. Make sure you have thought out responses to subjects you would expect to be asked so they come out naturally and relaxed. By hearing your responses, you will know what to change and what you need to work on. Yes, it may be awkward at first, but you'll understand what I'm saying as soon as you give it a try.

Now all of this information and guidance will help you tremendously, but I'd like to include just three more things.

1. The most basic question you can expect is, "Tell me about yourself."

> Not really a tough question, or is it? The interviewer is asking for you to fill in the blanks. Sounds easy right? However, in my experience because it's so general and open, many get flustered by it and don't know how to respond. Let me help you out.
>
> The inclination is to start with academics and school because that is forefront in your mind and what you think they want to hear.
>
> However, that information will be on your transcript and on your application.

It is not that it is not important, but I feel the interview, as with the essay as we discussed, is a time to talk about you and who you are.

So, I always suggest you start with personal information like your family, the fact you have a dog, or that you are close with your grandparents. You could eventually address your academic favorite subject, potential career or major interest when asked.

However, in an interview, when asked to tell them about you, I believe you start with personal, non-academic information first to break the ice, show you are comfortable and maybe even to find commonality between you and your interviewer.

2. Expect the unexpected and have fun with it.

It is possible you will get a random, "out of left field" question to see how you react, how creative you are, and if you can handle pressure.

Some examples I've heard over the years are below, but obviously, it can be about anything.

- If you were a fruit, what fruit would you be and why?

- If you can sit with any historic person who would it be and why?

- If you could have any superpower what would it be and why?

- If you could travel anywhere in the world, where would you go and why?

These questions are for fun as well as to challenge you to think on your feet. If you have to buy yourself some time, do that by saying, "Wow that is a really interesting question. I've never been asked that before." Think about it for a minute, don't delay too long, but take the time to think about what you want your response to be and make sure it's a thought out, good answer. Then just go with it.

Also, relative to these types of questions, try not to give responses that are too common or try too hard to be different. I was asked the fruit question above twice in my life. Once when I interviewed for a resident assistant position in college and once in my big interview that landed me my corporate America job I told you about before. By the way, my answer if you are curious was a kiwi. Hopefully one day I will share with you the reasons why I chose that fruit instead of others, but for now I am going to leave you hanging.

3. Don't leave an interview if you think you messed up.

If you answer a question and immediately afterwards, even though you move on to other subjects, you start thinking in your head, "I really screwed that one up", then write it down on your note pad (because you obviously brought a notepad with your questions for the interviewer written down on it as well as some key reminders for yourself. I know I didn't need to tell you that but just in case....).

Then when you are asked if you have any questions at the end of the interview which is highly likely, say "Excuse me, I do have a couple of questions but before I ask them can I please go back to one of my previous answers to clarify my response?" Or something like that.

Of course, they will allow you to do so. Go back and address the question as you wanted and make sure you corrected whatever it was that you may have messed up. That way you walk out of the interview knowing you did your best. As I have stated several times, the interview will not likely be the reason you do or don't get into the college of your choice.

However, it can add to your confidence and mindset knowing in your heart and mind that you've done as well as you could possibly do to position yourself for strong admission consideration.

Russ' Rules... For Staying Cool

1. Know that you can't screw up your interview.

As I said, if you prepare correctly, be yourself and follow the guidelines I provided, you cannot and will not mess up the interview. Prepare properly, dress the part, be honest and open, don't let your interviewer make you feel paranoid, and follow up afterwards.

You got this!

2. Prepare correctly, don't just show up.

I don't want you nervous or anxious about an interview for any other reason other than the fact that you want to do well and make a good impression. I still get nervous when I am about to give a presentation despite how many times I have done it and despite how comfortable I am with it.

That is OK. But I know I am prepared and you should know that you are too. Do your research and practice your responses (out loud, in front of a mirror. Sorry to be annoying here but it is just so important and helpful).

3. **Have the proper mindset before, during and after the interview.**

> You can already tell I am a big mindset guy. I feel the right mindset is critical for everything in life. Have confidence you are prepared before the interview, have confidence you are doing well and can recover from any slip up while in the interview and walk out when you are done knowing you did the best you can. Impressions can be made not just by your specific answers but also by the way you handle detours and speedbumps. Show your maturity, confidence and flexibility by staying cool and going with the flow.

Eat, Sleep(?),
Think College, Repeat

"I love what I do. I am a lucky guy."

Russ

The alarm clock goes off at 6 AM but I usually don't need it. Sleep is a lost commodity most nights, but that's okay. Usually I don't need much sleep because I am charged up about what I do every day. That may sound silly but it's true. I know every day I'll be meeting with clients with new goals, aspirations, challenges and desires. Talking to them about these things, hearing their thought process and helping where needed is what helps me love my job every day. The uniqueness that each client brings to the college process, one that is somewhat regimented and calculated, provides sweet irony. It certainly keeps things interesting.

I always knew I wanted to help people and make an impact. I'm sure there were several personal upbringing reasons where this all came from, but we don't need to get into that right now. Helping people with one of the most challenging, uncertain, stressful and expensive endeavors of their life motivated me to start this business but has also continued to motivate me to help as many kids as I can.

Don't get me wrong, there are many people who don't understand why a family needs someone like me and I can't always disagree.

I have several friends who have tried to do college advising where they live and unfortunately, they have not made it. Not because they weren't knowledgeable, but because most families where they live are perfectly happy going to a local, state university.

Obviously, there's nothing wrong with that. As I said earlier, you don't necessarily need to go to an elite private school to be successful in life.

It's about *fit*: academically, socially, environmentally, geographically, and financially. It's also about what a student makes of their time at college as far as academic achievement, social involvement, and networking. It is also about the student taking advantage of all the resources and opportunities provided to them while at their school.

But in the competitive world we live in, where everyone wants to "get ahead of their neighbor" there are families that want competitive colleges on their list because they believe it will put them in a better position to achieve this goal.

They may or may not come to realize eventually that the college process is not about everyone getting a trophy, and that no matter what college a student attends, if they pay attention to the factors I listed above success is still possible. But many feel that attending a more selective college will give them or their child a significant advantage. Both scenarios are true by the way, as we have discussed.

However, when it comes to competitive schools, with challenging selection criteria, there are many variables that come into play. Making the right decisions regarding the various aspects of the process can and will potentially impact the end result.

I help these families and students become educated on their options, so they can make informed and intelligent decisions. Hopefully, with my advice and guidance the informed decisions they make will help them improve their chances for admission.

By the way, it is important to note that regardless of the actual admissions outcome (because I can't guarantee anything in that arena to my clients) one of the things that I love most about my business is seeing families and students evolve as they go through the process. I see them become motivated when they started the process timid or fearful. I see them lower their stress levels and actually add some fun on a daily basis.

I see them aim high but come to understand there are many great schools out there and they will excel if that is what they want to do, regardless of where they end up going to college.

So, every morning as I wake up I know unique interactions and experiences are on tap. Most of my clients have my cell number and I encouraged them to text me anytime, anyplace if they have a question, or are feeling overwhelmed, or need my help. I've done this, meaning helping students and families go through the college application and admission process, 1000 times literally. But I know they haven't and that they need to be talked off the ledge at times or pointed in the right direction or assured that they are in a good place. My daughter is used to me being on the phone or having to text a client at any time of day or night. She never complains and if I am driving she actually texts for me sometimes because she knows it is part of life. She hears how I help people and she also knows I love it.

Parents want to know they are doing all they should and need to do so they can avoid big mistakes and any feeling of guilt with the end result. Students want to know that they are not behind and that they will not miss any critical dates. Because there is so much information out there and so many people offering their "help", it is easy for them to get overwhelmed. That's where The Cool College Guy comes in to keep everyone calm and reinforce that we are where we need to be and will get to where we need to be.

As I make my morning coffee (and my first of five or six meals a day), I plan my day and review my upcoming appointments, identify if there's anything specific I need to do to prepare and make my list of phone calls. Then I head to the gym where I make these phone calls on the way. Calls to clients, potential clients, to colleges and others as needed. "Car University," as many people call it, helps my productivity and also helps me to be able to become educated on things I don't have time to sit and do during my normal day.

Gym time, though, I like to see as my time. I typically don't bring my phone with me and the gym is where my random thoughts about all kinds of things come up. Some people think in the shower, I think in the gym. Ideas about colleges for students, class choices, testing options, the athletic recruiting process, summer programs, you name it. Whatever is going on at the moment I think about and then make notes before I leave so I don't forget anything. It's what works for me and I often tell people my gym time is my meditation time. The one or two days I'm not at the gym during the week often puts me in an uncomfortable place momentarily because I am largely a creature of habit and routine as many who know me are aware.

But of course, I manage.

Anyway, believe it or not I would say about 75% of my clients are very engaged and communicate with me on a regular basis. Sometimes it's overkill with parents and students who overthink every decision they need to make. Sometimes they act as if their final college decision will be absolutely impacted by whether or not they attended a summer program or continue a fourth year of soccer when they can't stand the sport and sit on the bench every season. These clients always concern me not because they won't get into college, but I wonder if they'll ever be happy.

I wonder if they will ever be able to make a decision without causing themselves tremendous stress. I talk to them as needed and I often share my reasonable, cool approach to explain their options. I even make suggestions if they ask for them. I mean, I get it. Sometimes it does feel like every decision is critical, so my expertise and guidance is happily given and it is where much of my value is shared. I actually love doing this part so believe me I am not complaining.

But my clients who I have to chase every month to make appointments and ensure they are making progress through the process, they are another story. These are the ones that I spend a lot of my time worrying about. They're the ones who will be nervous and panicked when they didn't have to be. I want them happy and stress-free if possible.

So, I think about what I can do and call them to make sure they know I want to see them as well as to get an update on where they are and how I can help them. Some people get it together and become more engaged while others it seems just can't operate any other way. I always tell my clients no one has ever or will ever be left behind and it is true. However, to make the complicated easy you need to be engaged and take action when needed.

There's no reason to make the complicated, more complicated right?

Now I think about other things, business and personal, but I really do spend a lot of time where clients randomly come into my mind for various reasons. I love what I do and feel I am very knowledgeable regarding all things college related. However, I mention stress levels, anxiety, uncertainty, and mindset because I feel this is a much bigger part of the process than it needs to be.

Maybe it's my Cool College Guy approach to college and life that seems to make my clients feel much better? Maybe it's my general attitude that all is manageable and doable regardless of the challenges and obstacles that we are presented with? Maybe it's because I've seen the results as well as the details of many journeys through the college process and realized that nothing, and I mean nothing, goes exactly as planned?

But that's life, right?

Why should college and the college process be any different from what life is about? And maybe that's why there are such disconnects when difficulties are presented and happening to many families? Because we (as parents) want our children to get what they want so badly that we try to act as if life forces and dynamics don't apply. Then there's the pressure students put on themselves which is often from outside sources that makes them feel like any deviation from their "plan" could prevent them from successfully arriving at their college destination. None of this is true of course.

I spend a lot of time reminding people how amazing they are and reassuring them that they will be successful no matter what their GPA, SAT or ACT score is, or college acceptance letter says. It's what I spend about 50 to 60% of my time doing when I advise and consult families. The other time is spent on logistics, process, and strategy. The time I spend on mindset adjustments and managing expectations is critical and where I find my relationships with clients really reach another level. It makes their process complicated at times but it's my strength to help them sift through that to make it easier and I love supporting my families.

Helping them through these times, and my success in doing so, is a lot of what led me to write this book as well as to launch my public speaking business (www.russvitalejustsayin.com[iii]) where I do speak about various aspects of the college planning process. However, I also speak about the importance of youth, and adults, knowing how to make successful transitions in their life. I speak about mindset and overcoming the stories that we have convinced ourselves are true about who we are and what we will or will not be. I have found my years consulting families has made me very well prepared to address these areas with people. Sharing this passion and gift is a tremendous honor and I love doing it.

Anyway, though we already talked about the essay process I would like to go back there for a minute or two. During essay time, I think about each student I have. I wonder if their essay really is a good match for them to communicate what they are about outside of their application and transcript. As I said I love this part of the process because most students dread doing their essays. Most kids don't like to write and certainly don't want or feel comfortable writing about themselves.

But I love getting to know my students on another level and on a much more personalized basis. This is where much of our bonding takes place. This is where they share private thoughts, challenging aspects of their life and goals.

It's from this process that I watch my students embrace what's going on, often watching them go from discouraged and potentially unmotivated to inspired and, dare I say, excited about their essay(s) and college process.

This is where parents see my true value, not just in the college process and project managing that for them, but also in relating to their student, motivating them and bonding with them so they feel supported and they understand all the emotions that accompany this process are very normal.

I also mention essays because they also keep me up at night. Are they writing about the right topic? Is there enough about them in the essay? Are they trying too hard to be different? On and on. Typically, I wake up at 2:00, 3:00, 4:00 AM and think, "Wow I need to change so-and-so's essay topic." I take these essays very seriously as I said in the essay section of this book, and I can't rationalize an essay that I think isn't up to par. **I feel every student has a story to tell and I'm very good at finding something from nothing, and then watching the lightbulb in the student's head get brighter and brighter with every revision we do.** It's one of the most fulfilling things about what I do despite how labor-intensive and draining it is at times. However, I believe it is my genuine caring and ability to relate with them on all levels (academics, testing, athletics, music, food, workouts, just about anything and everything) that enables them to share and show their best. I love this part of my business and it's why I tell everyone, "I don't work a day in my life anymore."

Another thing that keeps me up at night are students and families visiting highly selective or name colleges when a student has little or no chance of getting admitted to them (or a family won't be able to afford it if they are accepted). I understand the desire to follow the crowd as it is human nature to see name schools that are going to impress others when you share them. We discussed this previously.

But I also wonder why a family would go visit these types of schools when their chances of getting in, affording it or both, are so slim? It wasn't at my urging, I know that for sure. As I stated earlier I specifically discuss this with my clients directly, so they know what a reach, match and safety is. However, despite these conversations, people enjoy mentioning the big, popular names and I can't really tell them not to bother.

Now for me, it's tough to balance this because I would never want to say a student cannot get into a school. At the end of the day, it's a very subjective process as we discussed.

So, I struggle between saying, "You have no shot", which I would never do and letting them continue to go to high-end schools that I know are highly unlikely. When I know in my heart and head that the reality of them being accepted is slim and the reality of them being potentially disappointed is great, it pains me.

I tell them the truth as nicely as I can but that doesn't mean they always listen. So, I spend a lot of time thinking about what I can help them with and how I can communicate to them what their potential is, without discouraging them, and keeping them motivated. This is also where I emphasize a great Plan B as we covered earlier.

I know it is sensitive for all involved. I feel I need to address these things because I never want a family to come back to me completely disappointed. Obviously through the guidance I provide I do all I can to try to improve their chances and keep them on target.

I also advise them of what I believe are great next tier schools where they have a better chance of being accepted regardless of their academic performance and standing.

Every student and family need the right combination of safety, match and reach schools that include a great Plan B. I always take time to address this and find what will be, in my opinion, very solid choices from all the aspects we discussed together.

This is in case their first-choice school doesn't say yes. As I tell everyone, "You don't come to me to be late and you don't come to me to be wrong because you can do that on your own." However, I have to balance my directness with my clients, so they can aim as high as they wish but also know the reality of their given situation. This is challenging but I do it and I think I do it well. It's all about the delivery and ensuring that we will do everything we can together to get the best outcome while also managing their expectations and offering solid additional options.

Not everyone appreciates my honesty, and, in those cases, we collectively agree we are not a good match. Thankfully this happens rarely. In the free 45-minute consultations I do with families, I share my approach and philosophy clearly so all expectations al mutually known. I find this helps tremendously.

So, there's much that goes on in my mind when I work with families. I want them to have a good experience. I want them happy with me and my services. I provide comprehensive services that will address their every situation.

But most importantly, I want my families to be happy because they know I care and have done everything I can to support and aid them throughout the academic, financial, athletic and psychological process. It may sound like I am exaggerating but

I promise you it's true. I left corporate America and created this business to have purpose and to have an impact on others. I thought about, and still do on occasion, my own life experiences as well as how my life could've been different if I had received the guidance, caring and support of someone like me. It's not that I am not happy with where I am because I am.

However, if I had someone who believed in me, no matter what my numbers were or where I went to college because they saw uniqueness and strength in me would that have changed my mindset and path earlier on?

Hey, I am sure I wouldn't be who I am without the struggles I have had, so I am not sorry for them. But helping more people, earlier on, would have been nice. Also making what at times was complicated for me easier sure sounds like a great offer.

As I stated to you earlier, and it's one of the reasons I am sharing who I am with you, I am living proof that life doesn't always go as expected. But if you pivot and make transitions with confidence and positivity you can make it all work out. This is true with college and life. Okay, I will get off my mindset soap box now. Thank you for indulging me.

I feel that the whole reason I created this business is being solidified every day. This is especially true when families actually listen to me and take my advice. You may think that people would obviously do that, but then again you may be surprised. I tell everyone that I give a lot of great advice from my desk, phone, or computer. However, it is obviously their choice as to whether or not they want to act upon my advice or put it on the back burner for a later time.

The learnings and stories I have walked away with as a result of working with so many families have enabled me to help many others. I have even helped in many different capacities, whether it is in college guidance, life coaching, mindset training, or just interesting party banter.

There are times when I am mentally exhausted at the end of the day, just drained. It can be taxing at times to go as deep as I do with my clients. But it's what I love to do and what builds the types of relationships that I know are lasting and that have a positive impact. That's been my mission and my passion. To be there for people who need my help, to connect with people on a level that is unique, authentic and meaningful.

It's one of the most amazing aspects of my business. It is what drives me every day. When I do this, life is good! And life really is good every day.

Thank you for letting me share this with you. I do this, so you can understand me a bit more. It is important to see where I am coming from, and how I have developed my approach to the college process that is now in this book. Hopefully my insight to what I think about and how much I genuinely care about people comes through to my clients daily and to you in this book.

Russ' Rules ... For Staying Cool

1. Every "job" can be challenging.

Every job change you make, or endeavor you pursue can present you with challenges. There is no way to avoid them because as we have discussed, life is fluid and rarely goes as you expect it to. I exert a lot of time, effort and caring into my client's college journey. However, as tough as it can be at times, I love every minute of it. I am an example that I described earlier. I am the guy who found his passion from a very unexpected path. I am proof that you can be happy and successful despite going through life with many detours and speed bumps. You can too. I wish that for you.

2. Life is a process.

Life is not a direct path. Navigate as best you can but don't let detours and speed bumps convince you that you are on the wrong path or not worthy. Whether it is college acceptance, job offers or personal relationships, stay true to who you are. You should know that you can accomplish what you want if you stay driven and know how and when to pivot. Transitions are inevitable. Don't fear them, regardless of what initiated them. Accept them, embrace them and enjoy them.

3. Gratitude is critical.

No matter what your goals are, be grateful for what you have and what you have achieved. It is hard to do in the fast-paced, beat everyone out world we live in. Reach for your best always and all ways but also take time to appreciate what you have and what you have accomplished. I am grateful for my daughter; the support I have from others and the privilege I have had (and hope to continue to have) doing what I can to be the Cool College Guy for the families I have served.

"Rejection" Can Be Your Protection

"Don't let speed bumps and detours knock you off course."

Russ

Rejection is in quotes above because there are several different forms of rejection. It can be outright in that a person doesn't want to spend time with you, you weren't offered the job, or you were not accepted by a college. However, in addition to this traditional definition, "rejection" can also come in the form of not getting what you think you wanted or what you expected.

Years ago, I was working in corporate America and I was in charge of a multi-hundred-million-dollar market. As a result, I traveled all over the country, not so much because they wanted me to, but they took away 20 of my salespeople and I was trying to retain our business as best I could. It sounds great in some ways and believe me it was (in some ways). Seeing the whole country on the company's dime was a great opportunity to visit exciting cities, experience their way of life and to meet interesting people. I did enjoy most of that, but enabling me to build relationships with people in the various regions within my company was also a great opportunity. They appreciated my efforts in the regions to help them maintain their revenue much more than my headquarters did, but that's a story for another day.

Anyway, as result of my efforts and results, I was offered jobs in all the regions at one time or another. I've been in the New York and New Jersey area my whole life and thinking about living somewhere else has been enticing for many reasons and for many years. However, for some reason I seemed to always come up with excuses to turn an offer down and stay in the Garden State. But then there was one offer that seemed too good to refuse similar to the scene in The Godfather (minus the intimidation, Italian music and cheek kissing of course).

Okay, so I am being a little dramatic but for me this was a big deal. I thought that maybe I might finally have an opportunity to experience life from another vantage point. For some reason (or another) this time, the timing, job, and personal circumstances all seemed to align, and I accepted a job in Denver, Colorado. It was a hard decision and I hemmed and hawed about it for over two months, but I finally accepted. Well, if you know anything about big Fortune 500 companies, they typically move very slowly. This is very much a hurry up and wait mentality. It is kind of like getting in line the night before tickets go on sale for a concert.

After some time, the hiring manager called me and said they had decided to go in another direction and add the job responsibilities (that they had offered to me) to an existing position rather than hire me for it specifically. I was devastated! I finally made this decision, was looking forward to it and started telling people I was leaving only to have it pulled from under me. Now what? Well two months later the company reorganized yet again and shut down the region I was going to move to in Denver.

All employees had 90 days to find a job, inside or outside the company (didn't matter), or relocate to another region of which

New Jersey was the main consideration for most of them, because that's where all the jobs were. It turned out what I thought I wanted, and I was upset about losing, was actually a blessing in disguise.

In the college process whether it's trying to get into an AP course in high school, or playing sports, or being accepted to a top choice college, there are intangibles that happen. Don't get me wrong, no one likes rejection in any context. It feels lousy. Asking someone to the prom for them to say no (although nowadays there's so much gossip and hype before someone is asked, with elaborate proposals, so most know the result before they even ask), or being cut from an athletic team, or not getting into the colleges on your list, can be devastating at first.

How could they not want me?

Why would they take her instead of me?

I am much smarter than he is.

I am not going to be successful now.

On and on and on.

But as we discussed, sometimes as they say, one door opens when another one closes and sometimes if you play it right, many doors open. It turns out that sometimes not getting what you thought you wanted is the best thing that could ever happen to you.

You may have heard this before:

*"Life is 10% what happens to you and
90% how you react to it"*

Charles R. Swindoll.

Despite the fact that we have heard this saying many times before, we often treat sayings such as these like clichés. When we hear people say this to us, we think, "Easy for them to say because they're not the one going through this." But most of the time the saying is true. To be clear, you're absolutely entitled to feel disappointed when something doesn't go your way. But bounce back! It's their loss. You know why? Because you are awesome! You're going to be awesome no matter where you go to college, and regardless of you not getting everything you thought you wanted. They (whoever "rejected" you) will now have to watch from afar and get filled with regret as you kick ass and take names.

From what I have heard, apparently 12 publishers turned down JK Rowling with her *Harry Potter* [iv] book series. Sylvester Stallone was kicked out of more director's offices than he can remember before he turned the *Rocky*[v] franchise into one of the greatest of all time.

There are lots of examples of people being rejected, but the stories of their accomplishments in spite of that rejection is what inspires us. Stay with the *Rocky* theme for a minute please – okay, it applies to *Undercover Boss* too. I watch *Undercover Boss* all the time with my daughter and 9 out of 10 times I get a little teary at the end because the underdog gets the help, support, and/or opportunity, that they never thought they'd ever get.

Don't make fun of me – I'm the Cool College Guy enough to admit this so give me that at least. The struggle, the reaction to the unexpected detours, and the ability to bounce back from not getting what we thought we wanted is what makes us stronger. It makes us prepared for the real world and enables us to be interested and interesting at get-togethers and at parties.

We decide we want something. We artificially build it up to be something much more, much greater than it typically is. We do everything we can to create criteria to support the decision that we made and validate our choices.

Are these things real? Who knows? You have just as much potential to get a wacky roommate who makes your first year experience a nightmare at the school you end up choosing to attend as you would have at your top choice school.

There's no guarantee that because you analyze the situation and think you made a good decision (which we will address shortly) that there will be a smooth sailing trip from there on.

The decision-making is hard but after it's made, that's when the real world and real work begins. There are many people out there, smart people, who thought things through, did research, spoke to others, yet they did not experience what they had hoped. Every year I have students I help go through the college process who start their college journey in August or September and come see me, urgently, by Halloween to tell me about their disappointments and struggles.

Life at XYZ college wasn't and isn't what they had hoped or what they had built it up to be. They come back to me looking for my consultation, advice and guidance, which they have trusted in the past to help them make decisions.

By Russ Vitale "The Cool College Guy"

This time it is to evaluate whether or not they truly are in the right place. They need to figure out if they need to give it more time, or if it's time to move on and go through the process in a different way.

Your college journey, your life, is always going to be what you make of it. That will always be the case. I share that with my students all the time. It's a concept that many of us avoid whether we're young or an adult. We like to blame other people for unhappiness and dissatisfaction. We like to think that it has nothing to do with us unless it all goes perfect.

When things aren't perfect, that's when we look to blame others. But at the end of the day, is it not perfect because we made a bad decision? Is it not perfect because we didn't give it the effort that it really deserved?

Or did we make a good decision, yet things just didn't work out for us? Regardless, we need to take accountability. We need to realize that we have the strength and ability to make the experience the best it can be regardless of circumstance. I don't mean to change this into a mindset, self-help book. However, college is one of the biggest milestones in a family's and student's life as we mentioned.

It's not just about names and brands, but about finding the right place to thrive, as this book has hopefully shown you to do. But because college is such a significant decision that requires assembling a lot of moving parts, this flexibility and ability to pivot is critical in gaining the best possible outcome.

There are many adults that suffer from these same types of challenges. Once life throws a curve they cave, complain, and obsess over the "what if's?" Don't let that be you... ever!!

You deserve better and life is about making the most of the opportunities you have, not dwelling on those that haven't gone your way.

One college, one person, one job isn't what defines us or your ability to be successful unless you allow it to. Not getting what you want, or wanted, can actually be the best thing that ever happened to you.

Real Life Student Example of
"Rejection" is Your Protection

I had a student who has become one of my favorites over the years. I've been consulting and advising students relative to their college journey for almost 15 years and over this time period I have met many amazing kids, many great parents, and built relationships with many of them as we go through the process. Obviously, there are some I get closer with than others for assorted reasons, but many keep in touch to share with me how they're doing.

Many of them actually initiate the communication for the future because we built such a great relationship and because they like to come back to me to continue asking for my advice, ask for information that might help them to make whatever decision they're thinking about, etc. They end up realizing that the guidance I give them is typically very accurate and helpful, so why not come back for more, right?

However, this one student was a special case for many reasons, but I will not go into detail at this moment. But in the true spirit of "rejection" being your protection I would like to share this with you. She had a favorite school that was her favorite since her very first visit on that cold Sunday. She felt it was and would remain her top choice, and it did.

Now in reality, she was an absolutely amazing student with very high ACT scores and a very high GPA, captain of a sporting team, performing in musicals in her school, volunteering, taking all the toughest classes, she was absolutely an amazing kid as well. But unlike many high-end students her top choice ended up not being an Ivy League or sub Ivy school.

It was a school that she thought was a good match for many of the reasons that we've gone through and discussed in this book. The only reason she did not apply early decision to the school was because she needed to be sensitive regarding financial aid. Since the school was one of the most expensive in the country, and her family's special circumstances were unique, she applied early action instead.

Long story short, as we go through the process and I advise her as I always do, she took my advice (and then some) to make sure that she showed interest in the school. She went to multiple college fairs and saw the admissions counselor for the school several times. They knew she was there, she had conversations with them at multiple events and she always wrote follow-up letters afterwards.

In addition, she visited the school twice more attending the information session and did a tour, as well as she reached out to professors on campus and did all the things that I suggest somebody would do, who is very interested in the school (it is called demonstrated interest). She even drove down to the far end of the state to attend a special event the college was hosting and once again saw this admissions counselor, spoke with them directly and sent another letter as a follow-up.

After going through the process and waiting for an extended period of time to hear the status of her application (some schools are absolutely ridiculous in their delayed responses for acceptance or not when you don't apply early decision. Many allow kids and their families only 2 to 4 weeks to make a final decision which in my opinion is absolutely not fair). Anyway, she found out from the school that she was actually waitlisted rather than accepted.

We were shocked. She was devastated! We spent much time on the phone discussing things and I explained to her why I thought it might've happened. However, I also did tell her that I would make a phone call on her behalf. This is something that I do but only in certain circumstances. In general, I do not believe that I should get in the way of admissions decisions, nor do I ever try to lead somebody to make an admission decision.

Overall, I believe that the people who are in admissions obviously understand their criteria and typically do a pretty good job of picking the students that are right for their community and their school. However, in this instance, I was very upset, she was very disappointed as well and I could not understand how this could happen. So, I did make a phone call.

I asked some generic questions of the admissions counselor, made sure that from an academic perspective my student was evaluated correctly. We also discussed all the activities and different things that she's involved in to make sure that (once again) the school had evaluated her accurately. What the admissions counselor told me was that everything looked great from an academic perspective on paper. "She looks like she would be a great match for the school." Those are actually the words they used.

So, what was the problem? The counselor said she showed a lack of "demonstrated interest." What?? Are you kidding me?? That was what I wanted to say although I tried my best to keep that in and I said, "Okay, please, there must be a misunderstanding?"

I went on to then tell this admissions person that in addition to all the different visits and things that the student has done, she also wrote 18 (yes 18) essays for this school.

If that's not demonstrated interest, I don't know what is. When I mentioned that, the admissions counselor said, "I'm a little confused. How do you get 18 essays?"

This school had a common app essay, a supplemental essay, essays for their Honors program and also essays for a specific scholarship that they offered. She wrote every one of those essays, after doing thorough research and spending a lot of time writing them until she was happy with them.

He told me that they don't look at those essays when they make an admissions decision. They only look at the Common Application essay and the supplement. Are you kidding me? The student spent hours and hours writing 18 essays. How is that not demonstrated interest and how do you not know she did that? How can you possibly fully evaluate a student's interest in a school without reviewing their complete application submission?

I was appalled. I was disgusted, and I was incredibly angry to be honest. It was obvious to me this school had completely mismanaged the admission process for this student. I felt that given this gross mismanagement, there was no way that the school deserved this student. If that were my child, the way they handled this situation would be reason enough not to attend even if they accepted her later on. There are enough schools out there that are just as good (if not better in my opinion).

This school would never be worthy of having a student like this on their campus when they have made this kind of huge mistake. But the question I had to face was, how is my student going to feel about this? I hung up with the admission person very upset, very disappointed, very angry, but knowing that now I had to make a phone call to my student.

Being sensitive to her and what her thoughts were about the whole process was important regardless of what I thought.

I spoke with her and I told her about my conversation. I tried to keep my emotions in check and make it as much about business as possible. However, this is a student that I built a very close relationship with. She did take a little while to come out of her shell because she is a more reserved person, but we had bonded considerably over the time we had together.

So much that at one point she was texting me almost every day with different questions, different status updates, and to be honest with you, despite the constant texts, I was happy that she was so involved and taking it so seriously. I loved being able to be there for her, especially given her situation and I really enjoyed watching her grow and develop over the time I spent with her.

In typical Cool College Guy fashion, I treated her like she was one of my own. I wanted that for her, for her dreams, for her goals, and for her efforts. After we went through my whole conversation I explained to her what happened. I told her I was really sorry and that this should not have happened. It was a gross mismanagement by the school and at this point she could wait on the waiting list, but I didn't know what else there was for us to do.

After a brief silence she said to me, "You know what? The hell with them! If that's the attention they gave to me and to my application given all that I presented to them then you know what? They obviously don't value me and therefore they do not deserve me!"

I have to tell you I couldn't have been happier. Of course, I originally felt terrible about her situation. However, I was now relieved that the student felt the same way I did. In addition, the growth that I had witnessed from this young adult (not all my doing by any means although I do believe that my coaching over the time I spent with her hopefully helped) to make a decision that I felt was mature was impressive. She made a strong pivot from disappointment to looking forward to her other opportunities.

To see her do this without me egging her on was absolutely gratifying and so amazing to witness. She had many other offers from other schools that were very, very good schools. By the way many were even more selective in every way. Now it was her decision to take control of her situation and not be at the other school's mercy. She made a great choice and she is going to a great school.

She was also accepted into the other college's Honors program and given a lot of money to boot. She was excited, as you can imagine, to begin her college journey in that school and has had a tremendous experience thus far.

I share this story because here is a student who absolutely had her heart set, almost from the time that I started working with her, (throughout two and a half years). Every conversation we had seemed to somehow come back to the fact that she thought that this first school was her top choice. It was in her mind, it was in her heart and then something like this happens that's completely out of her control. It shakes up what she thought was going to be the norm, what she thought was going to be a done deal.

There are many ways she could've reacted to this, and some of them may have been ugly. She sat back and realized that this rejection of her expectation, this disappointment and this complete change in what she thought was going to be her reality going forward, was actually a blessing in disguise. It doesn't mean she didn't feel emotion about it because she did. It doesn't mean that it wasn't tough for her at times and that she didn't cry in the beginning, because she did, and I don't blame her. But she got composed. She thought it through and realized that she deserved better.

She understood that maybe she had built up in her head that this place was much better than it actually was. Maybe the true colors were now showing at this point in the process and pointed her in the direction that she really needed to go.

Everybody reacts to things differently. I understand that maybe you would or would not respond or react the way this student did. But all I can say is that when we hear and see these kinds of examples, day in and day out, of people thinking they want something, convincing themselves that they want something, and then not getting it, it is an opportunity for more than just disappointment.

Despite the struggle, the rationalization that you need to go through, the frustration, and anger or sadness that you may feel, will lead to knowing you can and will overcome it. Most times your new path will be even better for you if you approach it in a healthy manner.

Reevaluate and look at the situation on a holistic basis, not from a "why me?" perspective. Allow yourself to feel what you need to but limit the time for that reaction and move on. Hopefully as I have seen over and over again, you can actually be happy with what you do have. It is important to realize that there are many great opportunities (and potential) within those things that don't go as we expected. Choose to make the most of it!

Thankfully this does not happen very often. A large majority of my students have results that are close to what we expected. They also have very successful journeys if they take my advice and have reasonable expectations. This student in my story ended up having this as well despite the detour she ended up taking.

The illustration above is just an example of the crazy things that can happen as you go through the process despite doing all the right things. The most important thing to know is that it's not your fault. In addition, know that you can and will be okay if you stay cool.

As I said, most of the time things pretty much go as expected for my clients. I am candid with them and we work closely together to make sure that we do all we can to get the results we expect.

However, the college process is very subjective.

No matter what you do or what your numbers are, it is possible that you may get an unexpected surprise (some positive and others like this student story I shared). Regardless of which one happens to you, it is important to understand that things really do tend to happen for a reason. Embrace your altered path and make the most of it. Sometimes "rejection" is truly your protection, sending you on a better path.

Russ' Rules... For Staying Cool

1. Make goals but stay flexible.

It is important in the college process, and in life, to make goals. That is how we progress and reach heights we never thought were possible. However, sometimes things don't go as planned. Sometimes because of things we did or didn't do, and sometimes we do the right things, but it just happens that way anyway. Learn from the event and go through the emotions and thought process you need to, so you can then move on quickly. Not getting what you thought you wanted can actually provide other opportunities and set you on a path that is actually better for you.

2. Understand that you cannot control everything.

As with the student story I shared, it is true that despite doing all the right things, sometimes the outcome can still be something other than you expected. We often cause ourselves more pressure and grief trying to control things that are out of our control. Do the best you can and be as proactive as you can. However, understand that in spite of that, things can happen that may impact the outcome in a way that you didn't want or expect. The sooner you realize that not all things will go your way, despite all the planning and effort you put forth, the easier you will be on yourself and the happier you'll be as you go through life. This is true for college admissions but also for so many other life experiences.

3. The college process is academic but also a psychological marathon.

I am including this because a big part of making the complicated easy is about proper mindset and proper expectations. There is a balance between pushing as hard as you can to aim as high as you can go and accepting the results. Accepting the results is not settling. Your standardized test scores may not be as high as you wanted. You may not get accepted into your first-choice college. You may not get the job of your dreams. But that is OK. Pivot and learn to make it what you want or wanted it to be anyway.

Parents feel pressure that other parents will judge them based upon the college their child attends. Students worry that others will not perceive them in a positive way if they don't go to a college that everyone is impressed by when they hear the name. This is only true if you let it be so. Don't do that to yourself. Your success and happiness quotients are up to you, not the opinions of others. Keep that in mind and you will not only have a successful college journey, but you will also have a positive life!

So, What Do I Do Now?

*"Making the "right" choice is often
more difficult than you might think."*

Russ

In the past I've dabbled as a football and lacrosse referee. Though I haven't done much of this in the last 5 to 8 years, when you're on the field you need to know that you are not there to be the focus of the game. Actually, the greatest compliment I found that you can possibly get is if, when the game is over, no one really even remembers that you or the other official were on the field.

Your main goal is to ensure there's no real advantage gained by one team, or disadvantage experienced by the other team. Either can, or will, alter the flow of play and can provide an unfair opportunity for one team over another. I share this because I will compare my role with families as similar to the role I played when I was on the lacrosse or football field.

Similar to being on an athletic field, when I guide families, I try to keep the process moving forward. I provide proactive guidance, so they stay ahead of the process, mediate when needed, and offer advice, so I can educate them on their options and guide them. This is all in an attempt to aid them, so they can make a good decision. I want to make sure parents and students aren't disadvantaged in any way; academic, social, geographic, financial, athletic, etc. Though my presence is more upfront on the field, my goal is really to objectively guide and advise my families, so they don't make any of the big mistakes many do, don't miss deadlines, don't miss opportunities, and maximize their options based upon their collective goals and objectives.

So, you will go through the process as we reviewed in this book, and hopefully you will keep in mind the things we've covered. My wish for you is that by doing that, you achieved application success, meaning that your student has several great options that they are considering, or that those of you who may have applied early decision to a school, had success and have been accepted. In that instance, I hope the information provided here helped, and that you, and your student are very happy, relieved, and excited about your destination next year. Congratulations and good luck!

For the rest of you who have not applied early decision, or who have moved on to Plan B, as thrilled as I hope you still are to have gotten several acceptances, and to have the options we talked about, you may now feel like you have the weight of the world on your shoulders.

What school do you go to?

How do you make the decision?

How do you know if you're making the right choice?

These are all important questions. I watch families struggle each year trying to figure out what they think their best choices for the student and family may be.

There are many specific circumstances and criteria that can be used, but I wanted to review my top factors that I feel are critical in making a final college decision.

We have talked about them throughout the book, but now I would like to go a little deeper, so you know exactly how I define each criterion.

1. **Academic Fit**. I see way too many people letting the perception of the school, and name recognition, lead their decision-making process. As much as I understand this for the reasons we have addressed throughout this book, I think that many do this because of two reasons. First, they don't really know how to evaluate (and measure) the choices they have, so they default to a name they feel is recognizable or better known. By doing so, they assume they have a better chance to be successful and get out of the school, what they hoped or expected. It's not different from making a hotel or restaurant decision based upon a name that you know, versus one that is not as well known. We all know in many cases it doesn't mean the name brand is better. In some instances, you may actually think the other choice may have advantages. (Have you even stumbled upon a no-name restaurant and found it was one of the best you have ever experienced? I know I have). However, even when the known brand is not as amazing as you think it is, you still gravitate towards the known entity rather than taking a chance.

Second, as we discussed, there is a perception management dynamic that occurs within the student and parent's minds. They think that people will be more impressed by one name than another. Despite the fact that many successful business people, and even athletes have come from lesser-known schools that aren't as common or popular, you think going with a name is the safer choice.

As a couple of examples outside the college academic arena, just to make my point, let's talk about a couple of famous and very successful football players. First look at Phil Simms. Do you even know where he went to college? (Morehead State University) What about Jerry Rice? (Mississippi Valley State University)

Jerry Rice is arguably the best wide receiver to ever play in the NFL. Phil Simms was a Super Bowl Champion and MVP. Neither came from powerhouse schools known for football. There are lots of examples of business people as well, that fit this mold. The most successful person I know makes more than $5 million per year, yet he went to a college hardly anyone knows when I mention it. However, I tell my clients two things. One, right now with what he does make per year, no one cares where he went to school. Two, they (the college he attended) obviously taught him something because he's very successful, and professionally happy.

Once again let me state what my experience has been. Name recognized colleges can absolutely be helpful and open doors of opportunity! They can also help you to meet people of influence. These things can make your college experience successful in many ways. This then can lead to further success personally and/or professionally. I have seen that happen and I am sure you know people where this is true.

However, brand name and recognized schools are no guarantee of the same. A less competitive school that was the right match, and environment, for a student, can also yield the same type of experiences and success. I have seen both scenarios over and over again.

This gets us back to our first key point which is academic fit. I tell my students when they are considering a school that is a reach for them, that I don't doubt they can do the work if they had to, and really tried. But the question is, do you want to just survive at the school you attend, or do you want to thrive? Thrive meaning that you learn a lot and that you can manage a challenging workload, while also having a holistic successful experience, which includes good grades, good friends, good experiences, and school happiness.

The type of student you are, how you function best when it comes to absorbing information and preparing for tests, support you may need when or if you struggle, and how competitive the academic environment is, can often lead to added stress. For many this dynamic could even impact the social dynamics of the school. Talk to students attending to get clarification on all these points, before you decide if a school is, or isn't a good academic fit for you. Don't go on assumed reputation because college, everywhere, is not high school. It is challenging and difficult for many no matter what college they attend. The degree of difficulty, and how the student responds to it, is the critical point.

2. Attend the Accepted Student Day events for schools you're considering once you are accepted. Not every school you are accepted to is worthy of you going to this event. However, for the top two or three schools you're considering, you absolutely should go to the event. However, please make sure you take a couple of steps that I am about to suggest, to ensure you gather deeper, real information. This is especially true if you haven't seen the college while they were in session (while students were on campus), or if it's been a long time since your last visit.

You have to know that at these types of events (Accepted Student Days) colleges roll out the "red carpet" and usually show you their best, because they want you to enroll, and choose them. So, you should attend the event and plan your time wisely to ensure you get the information required to satisfy your needs and curiosities. But you should also do this to compare the school you are visiting with your other top choices. But that's just the beginning

I advise my clients to set up appointments, before the event, with the resources necessary to help answer the questions they have. This may include financial aid, resources in or at several academic departments, academic support services, the career placement office, etc. Make sure that your expectations are met, and that your assumptions about access, process, reliability, and then some, are satisfied.

Lots of schools say they have a strong academic department in your major and that many kids had internships and the resources to help them when needed. But it's important that you verify these things to ensure there are no hidden surprises when you're on campus, and actually attending the college. Most schools will be happy to set these meetings for you, but due to volume, you should arrange them as soon as you know you will be attending the event. Don't wait.

Also, talk to students who are attending now. Not just those the college puts in front of you to tell you how amazing everything is. Walk around campus as I advised you to do during your first visit and ask pointed questions, so you know what the college shared at the event, is actually how the current student community feels about each criteria.

3. Major consideration. What will you major in and how will that help you move on afterwards? As we discussed, many students, even if they think they know what they want to major in, change their major multiple times as they go through their college journey. Therefore, it's important that the school offers a major you think you want to pursue, but also that there are options and flexibility if you should change your mind.

For example, most schools offering a competitive major in any of these areas, such as; engineering, accelerated medical programs, architecture, physician's assistant, physical therapy and sometimes even business, can often have higher standards for direct acceptance from high school into that specific program/major.

Therefore, if a student isn't accepted into the program they are interested in directly, it is important to find out if (and how) they can pursue their top major in the future. Sometimes that won't be an option at all and you need to understand that fact. That could be crucial to understanding and making a final college choice.

One school where you can or will be permitted more freedom to pursue the major you wish to pursue, and/or the flexibility to change your mind, versus another that is more strict in how they manage their students. This may be a great reason to make one college your top choice, and the other a distant second.

4. Social fit. I tell all my students that they need to remember that they are going to college not away for a four-year vacation. This is especially true of my students who say they want to go to school down south. I realize that a majority of my students live in the Northeast, and they would like to go to college somewhere else, for better weather. For some of my students, they say they want to go to California to get out of New Jersey.

I understand how they feel because I would like to live

somewhere else at times where the weather is always sunny, possibly with a beach close by, and no snow. But at the moment, the best place for me to make a living is where I am. Don't get me wrong, as I shared earlier on, I have always been a NY and NJ guy. I love it here for many reasons. But as many do, I have been thinking more about being in a warmer climate at some point in the future.

Likewise, when picking a college, the same considerations apply. You have to have more than weather as a key indicator. In addition, when you go to a geographically different place, you have to take into account the types of people attending. I've heard many stories of tri-state area students going to school in a different state and having some significant difficulty with their transition. It can happen anywhere, but if you don't understand the environment they are going into, it can be much more challenging.

Let me share a quick story with you: A female student of mine went to a southern school and she was very excited. She had wanted a southern school throughout the whole process and couldn't wait to go. We talked as we went through it all, in our conversations and meetings, about the options that she had and the potential for different opinions and attitudes being present at this school.

The fact that she was very dark haired and dark eyed unlike many people she saw attending this college made it easy for her to standout, but not necessarily in a good way as you will come to see. As silly as that sounds, people, especially kids, do make judgment based on things such as hair color to decide if you do, or do not, belong.

Anyway, she was walking across campus with three girls she had just met in a class. They were having a very nice conversation (or so she thought). As they stopped to talk a little more, one of the girls asked her where she was from. She said, "New Jersey" without any hesitation.

When the three girls heard this, they literally turned their heads and walked away without another word. Not nice right? I tell all my students this story because there are examples of this in any situation. It could be where there are geographical differences, or where some other type of diversity exists. This could've happened in the Northeast if somebody from outside the Northeast attended a college in this area. This could happen if somebody goes to school internationally. This could happen in any situation where an attendee is "different" from the majority population at the specific college you are considering.

Therefore, you have to be aware of this and not be thin-skinned. I give other examples of in-state versus out-of-state treatment to my clients too. Finding "your group" is important, but you need to understand it may not be as quick as you may like it to be. It may take some patience and a thicker skin. In this instance, like many things in life, it's not just what happens and how people treat you, but also how you react to it. Your resiliency can determine your success factor in situations like these.

Also, it is important to know how the non-academic activities run, such as clubs, fraternities and sororities, on-campus activities and even various sports. You can't assume you'll be met with excitement and automatically accepted into these activities. Often times there are rules, guidelines, and traditions that may apply. Understanding them before you agree to attend is an important part of the process.

So, talking to kids on campus, asking specific questions about what clubs and activities they are in, and what the process was (as well as their current experience) is critically important. That way you can go in without having unrealistic expectations. Let's face it, as we have said before, the happier the student is with their school, and social environment, the better they will most likely do academically as well. The last thing you, as a parent, want to do is spend an exorbitant amount of time on the phone trying to calm down your child because they didn't get into any of the 4 activities or clubs they applied to. This makes finding their friend group(s) much more challenging and can negatively impact the student's transition.

5. Financial Fit. In my opinion, way too many people put this at the end of the process rather than upfront as I suggest. I tell people, if you were buying a house, car, or business, wouldn't you have to check to see what was affordable before you start going to dealerships and specific homes? Granted, college works a little differently, if you understand how colleges award and consider financial aid. Regardless, having the knowledge necessary to decide if the college could be within your financial range is very important.

Despite this fact, many families ignore finance, either because they assume they won't qualify for any aid, or because they don't want to admit to their child that finances will have an impact on their final college decision. As we discussed in prior chapters, when it comes to college, parents can also often let the wrong drivers run their actions and behaviors, or lack thereof.

The proper way to handle college finances is to get your EFC (Expected Family Contribution) officially calculated, and probably not on some financial aid estimator the college posts on their website.

I say this because many parents put wrong information into the programs, and/or the calculator could be formatted for a specific school regarding how they handle financial aid, rather than universally applicable financial aid calculations.

However, it's also important to know that you don't need to spend any or a lot of money to get your EFC numbers calculated. You just need to understand your finances (and tax return) and then use a qualified site, or counselor, to calculate this number for you. *Here is one I have used in the past,*

http://www.finaid.org/calculators/finaidestimate.phtml[vi]

Anyway, the point of this book is not to teach you how to calculate your EFC. Also, as I mentioned several times, I don't believe that because the college costs more, it is automatically better. Likewise, because the college offers merit money, doesn't mean it's not a good enough school to seriously consider. Unfortunately, this is a constant opinion of many students which is completely wrong. I mean, in any other area of your life would you say with absolute confidence that if they like me, want me, give me something, want to spend time with me, then I must be shooting too low?

It just doesn't make sense. There are millions of self-help books addressing these topics which we won't address here. But my point is, as I've said throughout this whole book, it's about finding the right school (or schools) so you can have a successful and happy college experience. It's not to stretch your family finances because you somehow think the more it costs, the better it is.

So, assuming you have done your homework and took my advice to ensure the schools you are applying to are within your budget, let's discuss how to measure the financial impact when making a college decision. First, you need to apply for financial aid. There's a FAFSA that every school accepts for financial aid purposes and you can find it at; https://fafsa.ed.gov/[vii].

There's also something called a CSS profile which is provided by College Board, and over 325 private schools typically require you to submit this as well if you apply to their school. There may be other forms required by a given school, but these are the primary forms to consider and know. They are available Oct. 1st of your student's senior year in high school, and should be completed sooner rather than later, to maximize your aid potential.

After you apply to colleges, and submit your financial aid forms, you will get an acceptance decision that may or may not include a merit scholarship depending on the school, and the type of match you are to that school. Regardless of whether or not this letter includes a merit scholarship, typically in the month of March of your child's senior year, you should get a financial aid award letter for each school you are accepted to. This will list the total cost of attendance and list what you have qualified for, so you know what the total estimated cost of the school will be.

It will break down the merit, grants, loans, work-study, etc., that you have been awarded (or not), so you can know what your financial responsibility will be for that given school.

Dollars are one of the more tangible decision criteria because either a college is affordable or it's not in most cases. However, at this point, you can compare awards and meet with the financial aid and the admissions departments of your top choice schools, to see if there are additional opportunities to get more money. You should do this regardless in my opinion to understand how and when the amounts you are responsible for are due. At this point you can also ask for an explanation of your award letter, so you know all the options available to you, so you can make sure you (the student) are being evaluated correctly, and to see if there are other options for you and your family that may help offset the cost of college. This does not impact your student's admission decision in the slightest. So, do not feel that you should not ask these questions. It's just smart to assess, ask, and understand the details so you can make an informed decision. Then at the end of the day, it is your choice if you think one school that will be $10,000 per year more than another is actually worth it.

Note: Here are a couple things to remember based upon my years of experience.

Get educated on how each school you're considering addresses financial aid, merit that may be available, need-based only policies, need-blind policies, and the like.

Don't apply early decision to a school without doing your financial homework and meeting with the financial aid and admissions office of the school before you apply so you have a good idea what to expect.

Have a family discussion regarding your college financial standing so everyone knows the range you need to be in to make the school affordable. It is important to let everyone know that finance is a factor before you apply.

This is even true if you are fortunate to not need to make it a driving factor, because the overall expense is significant, so everyone should understand the importance of making such a big money decision.

Students please understand that college is expensive! It's not your parents' sole responsibility to make college affordable. It's also yours to be the best student you can be relative to GPA and SAT or ACT scores, so you can qualify for the Honors program (that usually comes with money), or for merit scholarships that may be available at the schools you're interested in. These will help to offset the cost of college.

College is a family effort and decision in my opinion. Therefore, students need to do their part as well, to try to help minimize the cost of college.

If for some reason you do not qualify for money from the schools you are interested in, you may have chosen the wrong schools to apply to, you may not have been as strong a match for the school as you thought, and/or you may just need to understand that writing a blank check to a college is not something that your family is in a position to do.

Because the college offers you money doesn't mean that it's a bad school, or that it is below you, or that you are too smart to go there.

Ask the colleges you are considering what other options are available, if any, to make it more affordable for you before you decide to attend.

Parents, please do not leverage your standard of living or retirement for your child's college experience.

Unless they are guaranteed a huge paying job and have contractually committed to you that they will care for you, be reasonable. There are many options out there of great colleges. Pursue them all so you have financial options available.

Though there are many other criteria that you, and your family, could use based upon your own personal circumstances, these usually apply to everyone. If followed properly, they should help you to make a holistic, realistic, and responsible college decision.

Good luck!

Russ' Rules ... For Staying Cool

1. **There are many great colleges out there, did you find them?**

   If you followed the guidance given in this book, you had a balanced list that provided options for you in every way. All of them should have been good options even if some are a bigger financial or academic reach for you. Don't let bogus rating guides and hearsay from others, mislead you or convince you to make the wrong college decision.

2. **Did you define and share your family criteria for making a final college choice?**

   The criteria you use to decide if one school is "better" than another is critical. Make sure the criteria are important to all decision members and weighted appropriately. At the end of the day, it is up to the student to make the most of the opportunities they are presented with while in college. If they do that, they will be successful and happy no matter where they go. If not, no name, ranking or other criteria will matter regardless.

3. Get details, don't assume.

Research and talk to as many people at the colleges you are considering so you know, don't *think* you know, how they will support and treat your family and student if you attend. Ask specific questions so you become informed, and can validate your assumptions, and make intelligent decisions based upon accurate data. College is a lot of hard work and an expensive endeavor (financially, academically and mentally).

By Russ Vitale "The Cool College Guy"

What to Know Before You Go

"People think the goal is to get into college. But thriving in every way should be the goal."

Russ

Congratulations!!! I hope you found this resource to be helpful, add clarity and make the potentially complicated easier. Many families get caught up in the college process, the acceptances and denials, announcing to the world where you will be going and then enjoying your summer with your high school friends before you are shipped off to the college of your dreams (hopefully). I don't blame you. Your college decision is one of the most significant milestones in your life and you should be proud of your accomplishments. You should also be excited about your new beginning and all college will offer you.

You've taken the time to go through the various components of the college application and admissions process that are typically most pressing. I am thrilled to have been able to guide you and answer many questions you had about what to do and when to do it.

However, I am sure you know that there are many other things that can impact the journey for a student and family. We have covered academic, social and financial fit so much I am sure it is etched in your mind by now.

But this thing called life will also potentially impact your experience and I would like to take a couple of minutes to help you prepare, so you are ready to have a great experience and make college all you want it to be.

So, let's talk about a couple of things that you all should know, and expect, when it comes to the student's first semester (or year) at the college they've selected. Again, there could be many other factors that need to be considered based upon your specific situation. However, these are examples of the typical dynamics, in my experience, that impact almost every student in some capacity, at some point, as they make the transition from high school to college. My goal is to raise your awareness to these things, so you can proactively address them as a family. I also want you to be armed to handle them if they come up, so you can minimize their impact and continue on the bridge to the best of your life.

1. Free time and self-regulation.

Many students have gone through a majority of their academic career having a full schedule, and I'm not just talking about school classes. Between sports, club sports, dance, volunteering, extra-curricular activities, and dare I say, a job, most high school students are used to having most of their hours in a given day planned for, including weekends. As good as this may seem for assorted reasons while they are in high school, as you go through the college process, it can create a challenge for the student once they are at college. Not playing sports anymore and not having a schedule that has been made for them can be difficult to adjust to. It can be a significant change for you and may require transition time.

Therefore, when you start your college journey, it is very important that you manage your time well. You can, and should, do this by planning out your week including time for studying. I am serious. Actually, schedule it in your calendar so you are prepared when you go to class and when the first test comes around. Don't think that just showing up for class will be enough for you to excel.

In addition, one of the best ways to meet people with common interests is to find new activities to add to your schedule. It is easiest to include those you have been involved in, and that have been important to you, in the past. This can include club sports, community service or even activity clubs such as hiking. This will help so you don't have more unstructured downtime and it can also help you to meet your new classmates outside of the classroom. Not doing this can make it more difficult to meet people and can also lead to boredom. Boredom, unfortunately, can sometimes lead to poor decision-making and spending time doing things you shouldn't be doing because you have nothing else going on.

It's important for students to understand that it is now on them to not just go to class but work into their schedule the time they may need to study, or do what they need to academically, so they are in a position to excel in their classes. Also, it is important for time management and social reasons, which we will discuss further next. Finding activities will add some structured commitments to a schedule so they are not overwhelmed with downtime. I know this may sound silly to some, "being overwhelmed by downtime."

However, I hear time and time again from my former students that too much downtime can lead to making poor decisions. No one is immune.

Each Sunday afternoon, you should plan out your upcoming week. Schedule time to study, time to attend the big game, time to attend social and athletic club events and so on. Be efficient with your time in college just as you were in high school. Maintain that solid foundation for being efficient and effective in the classroom and on campus.

2. As a high school senior you are the big kahuna!

You waited four years to be at the top, and now you've made it. Everyone under you looks up to you, and you don't really need to work to be special. "He's a senior" is said all the time, and that's all you need, to declare your "instant celebrity" status to those around you. While that's a nice feeling because, let's face it, we all like to feel important, that won't be the case when you start your new college journey. Being the big kahuna is very important indeed, but this can lead you to a false sense of confidence going into your new college environment. Remember, you will be starting as a new freshman and others will have more experience than you and they will also have their group(s) established. But also remember, they were once you, so you can do this. You just need to take action.

So, what do you do?

First, you meet as many people as possible in your new environment.

That will be easier for some versus others. If it's not in your nature to talk to random people you don't know, the next step will be even more important. But regardless, you need to talk to people to find out what they know about activities, study groups, clubs, etc. That way you won't miss the opportunity to consider something that may be a great thing for you. These seemingly little, non-academic things can help you with the transition, and help you find your way sooner versus later.

Second, you need to look for clubs and activities that may interest you, and attend introductory meetings hosted by the group or groups.

This will help you meet people with similar interests, and help you learn more about them to see if you can, or should, pursue it further. This is not just a college thing, by the way. This is something that continues in your personal, athletic, and professional life as an adult.

I've attended many introductory meetings for professional and athletic organizations. Some I have joined, and some I have not. But regardless, I always learn by attending these meetings. Even if I decide a group is not right for me, I have often found that the meeting or people at the meeting have led me to other opportunities.

I always meet and interact with the people attending these things, so I can learn more about the group and the members. Many times, the communication I have there, turns into a friendship that continues despite me not officially joining the group. Networking, as it is called, is an important part of life, development, and growth.

Attend meetings and find the people who are like you, so your social transition can be smooth. Sports are often the most obvious thing that comes to mind, but there are plenty of additional opportunities that provide the same benefits. Research them, talk to people and give it a try.

An open mind can lead you to new opportunities you have never entertained before. It is one of the most amazing aspects of the college experience.

3. Given what we discussed above this will sound contradictory, but don't jump into things too quickly.

This is especially true for sororities and fraternities where there are often time limits that can force you to accelerate your decision-making process. But you need to try to make sure in your anxiousness, that you find friends, and fit into your new potential group. **Don't just find things to do to occupy your time and jump into things too fast.** Doing this could set you up for a poor experience.

If you do jump in and find that the decision you made wasn't the best for you, or you apply to join a group but are not accepted, don't be discouraged. Remember that if you give things enough time and effort things can often change for the better. In addition, if you are not accepted you can go back to the "rejection" can be your protection philosophy. As we discussed, sometimes a poor result can't be avoided despite how much planning and research you put into the process.

However, you can minimize the negative impacts by doing your homework prior to committing and then pivoting if you get a negative result.

Bottom line is: try not to rush into anything. **Make sure the decisions you are making are what is best for you.** Let things organically develop without putting pressure on yourself so you can find happiness and the right group(s) to enhance your college experience

4. Expect speed bumps!

Look, as I've said throughout this book, the dynamics of life are applicable to your college experience no matter how hard you try to prevent them. You may have a bad experience with a roommate, social group, athletic team, or academic class. This happens sometimes despite you doing your best preparing for it or trying to avoid it. **Don't let it discourage you or deter you from finding your happiness in your new environment!** Instead talk to people, and utilize resources provided by the college to help guide you towards a rebound.

Find options and activities to pivot, find new goals and endeavors. Learn and move on. I know you spent a lot of time celebrating and glamorizing the decision you made regarding which college you decide to attend. Good for you! As I said you should have celebrated because you earned it. You should be proud and excited. But don't let that buildup be shattered the second something doesn't go as planned. Don't second-guess everything you did and decide that because something went in a way you didn't expect, that you made the wrong decision.

If everything goes smoothly, good for you, you're very

lucky! But most likely there will be something that happens that deviates from the perfect world you created in your head regarding what college will be like. It can even be a small thing. A speedbump, or two, isn't an indication you made a wrong decision. It's the path we all go down every day in life. Therefore, expect the unexpected. Learn from it, and move on, to find your new way. Remember, as we discussed before, things not working out as you originally planned can be what prepares you for your future success.

5. Utilize the resources you have available to you during your transition.

These include resources provided by the college you are attending, such as academic support, writing labs, academic advising, etc. But this also includes personal resources like your parents and high school friends who know you well. They often can coach you through whatever it is you are facing at the time. It is okay to realize you need help, we all do! **How independent you are, or think you are, or want to be, includes admitting that you could use some help.** It is not a sign of weakness. It's actually a sign of maturity and intelligence.

You know when I left corporate America, one of the things I said that I didn't want to do was ever answer to anyone else again. Especially when that someone else had interests that were not aligned with mine, or where I was not at least a consideration in the process. I told you this, but it is important enough to restate it. I started my own business and I truly love it. However, I tell all my students, I can't just do what I want, when I want, all the time. I answer to my clients all day, every day. And if I don't, they won't be happy with what they've employed me to do for them, which is a bad thing.

I want every client I work with to feel like I was there for them when they needed me. Having them happy with the support and guidance they received from me as they went through the process is critical to my future success.

The bottom line is we all answer to someone. Independence is never 100% without any outside influence or impact. Understanding this and knowing that needing help, finding help, and working with others, is the best way for you to achieve your goal. Be aware that you need help or guidance. Don't wait too long to take action, or avoid it hoping it will go away. You'll be better off owning up to the fact that you need some guidance or assistance. It will be better for you in every way, so utilize the resources you have available, please.

Learning through trial and error is a good thing, too. Learning and improving through trial and error, getting outside confirmation, guidance, or help, is what brings learning to another level. So, know when you could use some help, find the resources that can provide you that guidance, engage them so you can receive what you need, and act upon the things you learn. And no, it is not a sign of weakness, but rather it's actually quite the opposite.

I'm sure there are other things that could impact your road to a successful transition and college experience. There are literally books written about how to do this as well.

However, I wanted to take a little time to address this, because as we have found throughout every chapter, *college is a fluid process and emphasizing making the "right" choice(s) is important.*

You can do this! The topics I mention above are to help you understand that college is not a continuation of high school. There are new, wonderful experiences in store for you, as well as new challenges. To help put you on the path to college success and happiness, these are what I have found to be the most common influencers over the years. I hope you take my advice, not as warning signs, but as additional awareness tools so you can improve your potential to have an amazing college journey! That is what I wish for you.

College truly can be the bridge to the best of your life. With focus, effort, common sense, flexibility, and action, you will improve your chances of crossing the bridge with minimal diversions. This will enable you to continue to find your passion, your purpose, and your happiness.

Good luck!

Russ' Rules... For Staying Cool

1. Getting into college is only part of the goal.

I tell all my potential clients during our consultation that I can guarantee, with or without me, they will be going to college if they are willing to pay for it. There is a college for everyone regardless of your GPA and test scores. Everyone focuses on getting in, and all that goes with that process. We have addressed that throughout this book, so I won't rehash all of that again. However, being successful and happy once you start your college journey is important as well. Do what you can to improve your potential for success, be realistic with your expectations, go easy on yourself so you don't apply unnecessary pressure on your academic and social status, and find assistance when needed.

2. Transitions can be challenging.

Life is about transitions. Some are for good reasons, or sometimes because we choose them. Sometimes a decision was made for us, or we didn't have another choice. The transition to college will most likely be one of the major transitions you experience in your life. As with any change you need to become informed, be patient and take action. Learn about your new environment. Don't rush to try to find your place. Take the action necessary to learn, meet people, find your group(s) and be an involved member.

3. Make the complicated easy!

Throughout this book we have tried to address the major aspects of the college process using logical, reasonable and realistic expectations. We have also tried to show that by taking the right steps, you can help make what seems overwhelming and uncertain at times, more manageable and attainable. Whether it is college or life, people sometimes tend to make things more challenging than is needed. They add importance to things without knowing if it will really matter. They use other people's opinions and perceptions to lead them, rather than doing what is best for them.

Try not to get involved in that game. The road to college is not always direct. It may contain speed bumps, detours and sometimes road blocks. In true GPS fashion, reroute yourself knowing confidently that you have arrived at your final college destination successfully. Once you get there, it is up to you to achieve what you are capable of achieving. You can do it!

You will be successful no matter where you go to college if you make smart decisions, if you optimize the opportunities you are given, and you take the right action when necessary. It doesn't need to be complicated.

Best of luck to you on your college journey! **I wish you much college (and life) success and happiness, always and all ways!**

About Russ Vitale

"The Cool College Guy"

Between his years at Corporate America and running his own company, Russ has presented to hundreds of audiences across the country ranging from small businesses, Fortune 500 companies as well as parents and students on many different topics.

Witnessing the changing world as well as the academic and social challenges facing today's youth, he created a college planning and placement company. His focus was to help high school students gain perspective and pursue their ambitions armed with the tools necessary to stand out and excel.

He shares his expertise, skill, determination, common sense, know- how, care and guidance to better students in all areas of development, help them achieve their personal and academic goals while also sensitively managing the expectations and anxiety of their parents. He specializes in relating to his audience by creating customized presentations and sharing targeted stories from his vast repertoire of professional and personal experience.

Russ believes that children are our most valuable resource. We need to cultivate them, model for them, teach them, learn from them and help them embrace their individuality to thrive. Russ lives in New Jersey with his fabulous daughter and enjoys life to the fullest. Russ is a cancer survivor which came unexpected as he has always made nutrition and exercise a priority.

The road to recovery taught him that life can change in a minute and one needs to live with a balance of making the most of today while planning for a solid future. In addition, Russ has overcome a challenging upbringing which taught him how to survive and flourish at an early age despite the obstacles he has faced. Fortunately, this has made him the strong, relatable and dynamic person he is today. People who meet and/or work with Russ know he is a 'Believer'. He believes that our success comes from the result of our motivation and inner inspiration but also our response to adversity. This is where he created his powerful talks on life transitions and knowing how to "pivot".

MEDIA RELATIONS

Russ Vitale "The Cool College Guy" can speak on many topics for your events, conferences or masterminds.

When professionally speaking, Russ can positively and uniquely command a room. His welcoming tone, presence and humor engage his audience. Through his relatable stories, vast repertoire of life experience and practical knowledge he enables his audience to take away actionable tools to shape their future and actively pursue their goals.

Russ is no stranger to speaking to audiences on a variety of topics. Recently Russ was inspired to share his perspectives on a more formal basis after attending Tony Robbins' "Business Mastery" seminar. Tony Robbins' "Proximity is Power" concept resonated strongly and became a driving force for Russ to incorporate this mantra in his life. As he shares his experiences and passion for helping others achieve their true potential, he motivates audiences to take action. Russ' energy and style are contagious, and the effects are impactful.

You can find out more about his public speaking interests by visiting www.russvitalejustsayin.com

For college guidance and advice please follow Russ on Instragram @thecollegeguy4you

THE END

References:

---

[i] Reference Disney's Lion King (The Movie)
[ii] From the official ACT Website

[iii] Russ Vitale's Just Sayin Page
[iv] Reference *Harry Potter*, (Warner Bros, JK Rowling)

[v] Rocky Balboa (Sylvester Stallone)

[vi] Calculating your Estimated Family Contribution (EFC)
[vii] Federal Government Agency for Applying for Financial Aid